You Can Do It!

Memoir Made Easy

What you need to write and publish your memoir

Karen Hodges Miller

Open Door Publications

Memoir Made Easy
What you need to write and publish your memoir

Copyright© 2024 by Karen Hodges Miller

ISBN: 979-8-9871697-2-8
All rights reserved
Printed in the United States of America

No part of this book may be used or reproduced in any manner whatsoever without the written permission of the author except in the case of brief quotations embodied in critical articles and reviews.

Published by
Open Door Publications
Willow Spring, NC
www.OpenDoorPublications.com

Cover Design: Emily's World of Design

To everyone out there with a story to share. Never lack the courage to tell the world about it.

Contents

Chapter 1
What Is Memoir? 1
Chapter 2
Why Write a Memoir? 7
Chapter 3
Who Are You Writing For? 11
Chapter 4
Set Your Goals 14
Chapter 5
Put Yourself Out There 18
Chapter 6
Hybrid Memoir and Memoir Plus 22
Chapter 7
The Arc of Change 25
Chapter 8
Organize Your Book 28
Chapter 9
Who Is Your Reader? 30
Chapter 10
Dialogue and Point of View 34
Chapter 11
Your Photographs 39
Chapter 12
Copyright and Disclaimers 44
Chapter 13
What Comes Next? 50
Chapter 14
Decisions, Decisions 55

Chapter 15
Beta Readers and Advance Readers 61
Chapter 16
Using Reviews 65
Chapter 17
Some Publishing Basics 72
Chapter 18
Amazon KDP vs. Ingram Spark.. 79
Chapter 19
E-Books and Audiobooks 85
Chapter 20
Marketing Basics.. 94
Chapter 21
Launch Your Book 101
Chapter 22
Keep the Sales Going 109
Resources 114
Acknowledgments 122
About the Author 123

Chapter 1
What Is Memoir?

> *Memories need to be shared.*
> — *Lois Lowry*

You've decided to write your memoir. You know exactly where you want to start. The opening paragraph has been written in your head for months, years, or even decades.

Now it's time. You sit down and write that first chapter. But where do you go from here?

In this book I hope I can help you think in news ways about your writing, your life, what you want to tell people about it, and then what to do with your memoir once it is completed. What lessons have you learned that you want to share with the world? What events were so compelling that other people need to hear about them? And finally, in what format should your memoir be written?

Some Definitions

The first matter you need to think about is what memoir is and what it is not. Many of the subgenres of writing about a person's life overlap, and while it may not be important to understand the subtle differences between some of these genres, defining them can help you reflect on exactly what it is you want to write about and how you want it to read when completed. Let's start at the very beginning by looking at the difference between fiction and nonfiction.

Fiction is a story invented by the writer. While some of the characters may be based on actual people, the story is not true. The author can take complete control of the characters and is in charge of what happens to them. **Nonfiction**, on the other hand, is *factual*. It is true—or at least it is as true as the author can make it. One person's perception and memory of events are often quite different than that of other people who lived through the same events. I'm not talking "alternative facts" here. I'm talking about the interpretation of facts. Two or more people often live through the same event, describe the facts in the same way, but interpret the events in a totally different way.

Let's look at a simple example that many people may have experienced: an auto accident. When I landed my first job in journalism at *The Butler Eagle,* a daily newspaper in Butler, Pennsylvania, I was assigned to the police beat. It was a smalltown paper that still published a daily list of all traffic accident reports, even the most minor. I was taught to always use the phrase "two cars collided" when writing up the accident, as in "two cars collided at the corner of Main and Brady Streets." The quick one-paragraph story went on to list the names of the drivers and if anyone was injured. The phrase "two cars collided" assigns no blame. It gives no interpretation of which driver was at fault. Changing the sentence to "A car driven by John Jones struck a car driven by Mary Davis" changes the entire slant of the story. And that was not my job as a newspaper reporter. My job was to just state the facts. Assigning blame was up to the police department that issued any tickets.

If this was a memoir written by John, the story might be told this way: "I was stopped at the red light at the corner of Main and Brady, just minding my own business, when out of nowhere this woman in a blue Ford pickup comes barreling around the corner and slams into my car. I did nothing wrong. I was just sitting at the light."

Now let's look at Mary's side of the story: "I was coming home from the grocery store and saw the light was turning yellow. I was really in a hurry to get home so I sped up just a little bit to make it through the light—and I did. I'm sure it was still yellow when my truck crossed into the intersection. That other driver jumped the gun. He started to move before his light turned green."

Luckily, we don't have to sort out the facts of this case. The fictional police officer in this fictional town has that problem—and I'm sure some heated words were exchanged between the two drivers before it was all settled. But I hope you see the point here. Everyone interprets the actions they see around them differently. This doesn't mean that one person is right or wrong. And it doesn't make one person's version of the story fiction and the other nonfiction.

Your job in writing your memoir is to make the story as true to yourself as possible. Often we think of nonfiction as being written in a dry, "just the facts" style that takes all the joy out of reading. While this style is just fine for technical, legal, scientific, and other factual writing, it does not lead to an interesting memoir. That's where **creative nonfiction** comes in.

What? How can nonfiction be creative? Doesn't creative mean that you have stepped away from the truth? No, it does not. *Creative nonfiction is factual material written in a way that tells a story.* While the writing style may be similar to a novel, creative nonfiction sticks to the facts. This is the old "show me, don't tell me" part of writing that authors must master if they want to keep their readers' attention and make them want to keep turning the page. If you've never heard this phrase, we'll discuss it more in Chapter 10. Writing creative nonfiction means that you write in a narrative style, and that you offer scenes, dialogue, and descriptions whenever possible.

Here are a few more genres for you to be aware of.

Biography: Biography is the factual account of a person's life written by another person. When we use the term biography, we often think of a birth-to-death account of the subject. This is not always the case, however. Some biographers focus on just one or two important events in their subject's life, while others try to encompass an entire era.

Autobiography: A factual account of a person's life written by the person themself.

Memoir: A factual account of a portion of the writer's life emphasizing one or two specific themes or lessons learned.

Portrait Memoir: This is an interesting type of work that is halfway between biography and memoir. It is the only case in which a memoir is written by someone other than the person it is about. For example, if you have found extensive material written by the person you are researching (diaries or other works where the person describes both events and emotions as well as experiences) You could write a "memoir" about the person rather than a biography. The writer must only include the subject's thoughts, feelings and actions without their own interpretation.

Hybrid memoir: This is a term some authors use to discuss a work that is part memoir yet combines it with other elements, such as a self-help or "how-to" work, inspirational messages, or even poetry. Yes, some very successful memoirists have used poetry to tell their story.

Historical fiction: This is another method a shy memoirist may use to tell their story while hiding the fact that it is true, and that the events actually happened. It can be successful for a number of reasons. It gives the author leeway to get to the existential truth of their message without worrying about strict adherence to the truth. What you must understand is that if you are writing a combination of historical fiction and memoir, you must make it clear to your reader exactly when and where you cross that line.

Using historical fiction techniques also allows you to use dialogue and descriptions for events in which you either were not present or for which you do not have a clear memory. You may want to describe events that happened before you were born, as I do in my hybrid memoir *Hibiscus Strong*. The book includes stories of events in my parents', grandparents', and great-grandparents' lives. Although the stories were told to me often as a child, obviously, I was not present when many of these events happened and cannot know exactly what my great-grandfather said to my great-grandmother at a specific time, or their exact motivations. For example, consider this excerpt:

"I don't like it. You know the Weather Bureau says there's a hurricane coming."

"Mary, the Weather Bureau is about as reliable as a chocolate teapot," Herbert scoffed.

His reaction didn't sit well with his wife. Mary sniffed loudly, trying to make the sound scornful, but he knew very well that she was trying to hide her tears. After almost thirty years of marriage, she couldn't fool him. Mary didn't like his job. Well, that wasn't strictly true. She used to like it. She had liked it until five years ago. That was when he'd switched from the Miami-to-St. Augustine run to the Key West run.

It paid more and it was only a half-day trip, which theoretically meant he was home most nights. He only had to stay over in the Keys if there was a problem. However, there were a lot of those. Even five years after its inaugural run, Mr. Flagler's Overseas Railroad was still called "Flagler's Folly" by most Miamians. And that was Mary's issue. The daily trip to Key West was dangerous.

Obviously, I wasn't present for this conversation, but I can make an educated guess about what was said and the motivation of the characters based on my knowledge of my family. This is the type of writing that adds color to a memoir. Your memoir is your story, and you can write it any way you want. So don't let someone else tell you that you are not writing memoir, or not writing nonfiction, if you add a scene such as this one. It is important to make clear to the reader, however, what you know as a fact and what you are making an educated guess about after researching your subject.

To sum things up, your story can be told in any number of ways. The important point is to lead your readers on a journey of discovery to the one important idea or theme that you want them to understand when they finally reach the end of the book.

Action Item

Think about your own story. What is the best way for you to tell others about it? Look over the types of memoirs listed in Chapter 1 and decide which is best for your story.

Chapter 2
Why Write a Memoir?

Write about small, self-contained incidents that are still vivid in your memory. If you remember them, it's because they contain a larger truth that your readers will recognize in their own lives. Think small and you'll wind up finding the big themes in your family saga.
— *William Zinsser*

"I'm going to write my memoir." It sounds quite pretentious, doesn't it? As if you were some really important and elderly person who, after a long and storied career, wants to write it all down so that others can learn from their accomplishments.

This, however, is rarely the case. I've worked with many people who were writing memoirs. The youngest writer was still in her twenties. When she came to me, I was skeptical that she had enough to say. But she was an expert in her subject—women's sexuality—with a very strong story to tell. Her memoir was quite successful.

Other memoirists I've worked with have included a World War II veteran, a man who escaped a Communist country as a young boy, a woman who worked with the United Nations in many countries, a person who had overcome dyslexia—and has gone on to write four more books, the mother of child who died unexpectedly at age 20 years, and many more. And these are just the traditional memoirs. The hybrid memoirs that come to mind include a book on sibling abuse, a couple of books on business success, a memoir written in poetry, and the story of a man helping his father through the last stages of cancer.

All these writers had different stories to tell; each of them were of different ages, genders and races. The one element they had in common was that they had lived through something that they wanted to share with others. They thought their stories could help other people navigate some aspect of their own life.

What's Your Story?

So why do you want to write your memoir? Is it for family eyes only? Or do you plan to publish it and make it available to everyone? There are many great reasons to write for yourself and just your family but having the desire to publish your work for others to read—to influence, teach, and inspire them—is a different game.

So before you begin to sit down and write that chapter that has been in your head for so many years, decide what your reason is for writing in this particular genre.

Have you learned an important life lesson that could benefit others? Have you been through a particularly unusual or dramatic event? Have you or a family member experienced a mental or physical illness that has given you information and insights that others can use? Have you come up with a new method for success that you know others can benefit from?

There are as many good reasons to publish a memoir as there are people who write them. There is only one bad reason to write a memoir: revenge.

If the only reason you want to write something is to get revenge on someone you feel has wronged you, don't do it. I'm not saying don't write the story; I'm saying **DO NOT** publish it. It will only backfire on you. If revenge is your reason for writing a memoir, take the pages you have written to a therapist and discuss your story. Then move on.

Standing Out

Thousands of memoirs are being published each year. The best way for your book to stand out in this vast ocean of information is to make sure that your writing isn't just average but is interesting, informative, and relevant to the reader.

There are no new ideas. This is as true of writing a memoir as it is for any other genre. Other people have written memoirs about their garden, their religion, their childhood, their marriages (both good and bad). With so much competition out there, you might ask yourself why you should finally go ahead and write that book you've always dreamed about. Other people have surely written something similar already. There really are very few new ideas in the world.

Don't let that discourage you.

Take a stroll through your nearest bookstore (yes, there are a few of them still out there), and you'll see entire sections of books devoted to the same topic. The internet has redefined the niche market. It is now much easier to find that small group of people interested in a very narrow subject.

Here are a few possible reasons for your memoir.

- You always wanted to write your story; you've had an idea in your head and an outline in your bottom drawer for years. This is true in my case. I decided to write a book about my family when I was eight years old. I even wrote that statement down in my diary. Of course, I didn't know the word "memoir" at the time; I just knew that someday I would like to tell my family's story.
- You know a better way. There are books on every business, every hobby, every passion. Some of them are strictly "how-to" books; others are memoirs or hybrid memoirs—a combination of a personal story with additional tips and guidance in following the author's path.
- You would like to become the go-to pro. Many successful business owners combine their personal experiences with tips on how the reader can emulate their success. With some marketing assistance, this type of book can make you the person that newspaper television commentators, radio hosts, or online bloggers call upon when they need to quote an expert in the field. Adding your personal story to a basic "how-to" book can make for much more interesting reading.

Action Items

What's your reason for writing your memoir? Answering the following questions can help you clarify your objectives.

- What would you like your book to accomplish for you?
- How can your book help you?
- How will your book help others?
- What other goals do you have for your book?

Chapter 3
Who Are You Writing For?

Don't try to visualize the great mass audience. There is no such audience—every reader is a different person.
— *William Zinsser*

Who do you want to read your memoir? Your children and grandchildren? Other family members? Friends? Or do you want to publish it and try to gain a national audience? The audience you plan on reading your book will affect the way in which you write it. Whether you are writing a private memoir or a public one, it is important to know your market.

If you are writing a book that is strictly meant for family and friends, you may not need as much of an introduction to the often complex relationships in the average family. But also, don't forget that even if this book is written for your current relatives, you also probably hope that future generations will read it. Make sure you are providing the necessary background information that makes your personal story compelling.

If you are writing for the general public, it is even more important to make sure that you know who you are writing for. If you've spent any time at all in business, you've heard the phrase, "find your target market." Your target reader is not everyone, or even "anyone who likes to read memoir."

Most people don't search for a book using the keyword "memoir" or "biography." They go to the bookstore—online or in person—looking for a book about a particular subject. It might be family relationships, gardening, how to start a business, medical issues, or any of a few thousand other topics. *They are looking for information.*

Let's think about someone who has just been diagnosed with cancer. They may begin by looking for factual information on their particular type of cancer but will also be drawn to personal stories of cancer survivors who can give personal, inspiring stories about how they conquered the disease. That is where memoir comes in. It gives specific information on one person's story that can help others learn and grow in their own lives. That's what makes a memoir special.

Before you begin to write your book, come up with as detailed a description of your target reader as possible. The more you know about your readers, the better equipped you will be in writing a book they will be interested in buying and reading.

Are your audience experts on your subject, such as your family members? Are they beginners in the field? This might be the case if you are writing a book on how to start a business or how to conquer a particular problem. Knowing whether or not your reader has background on your subject matter will help you adjust your vocabulary to the correct level. A book written for beginners that does not explain complex vocabulary specific to your subject will quickly turn off readers who are unfamiliar but want to learn.

Knowing who your reader is has a huge impact on how you write your book.

Action Items

Here are a few questions to ask yourself about your target readers.

- What is their gender?
- What is their age?
- What is their income level?
- What are their hobbies?
- What other books do they read?
- How much do they know about the subject of my book (i.e., is this written as a book for beginners or for experts)?

Write a description of your target reader. This person can be someone you know or a fictionalized, composite character. Either way, make your description as detailed as you can. When you work on your book, picture this person sitting at the table across from you. Write as if you are having a conversation with them.

Chapter 4
Set Your Goals

Setting goals is the first step in turning the invisible into the visible.
— Tony Robbins

How long have you been thinking about writing your memoir? You may, like me, have had it in the back of your mind for decades, or you may instead have only recently come to the realization that you have something to say and that the best way for people to hear you is through a book about your personal story. But it really doesn't matter where or when you decided to write your book. You may have written a few pages or made some notes, or you may have spent a lot of time planning your book in your head without ever actually sitting down to write it. What matters is now that you have made the decision, you don't allow your dream to gather dust in a desk drawer or a long unopened computer file.

Writing a book is difficult. If you've never written anything longer than a three- or four-page report, or even a ten-page short story, taking on a project as large as a book probably seems like a daunting task.

I have been writing most of my life; I've written short articles as well as long, book-length projects. I began my career as a newspaper reporter and editor, and only after several years of writing on a daily basis did I decide to strike out on my own as a freelance writer.

Over my years as a freelancer, other writer friends often asked me to edit the books they were writing. After working with several authors, I noticed a pattern. Many of the writers I worked with started their project with great enthusiasm, writing every day, getting up at 4 a.m. to finish a chapter, or staying up long after midnight. After a few weeks or months, their fervor waned. Real life intervened; the kids got sick, the job required overtime, a vacation or illness in the family disrupted the regular routine. The excuses were many and varied, and because they were invented by writers, they were all very, very creative. But no matter how creative the excuse, in the end it was always the same story: The book never got written.

A few of the people I worked with did finish their projects and went on to publish their work. Even though I began to work as a book editor for more and more authors, I noticed the success rate for finishing projects never improved; it remained about one in five. Then one day I got a call from a person who worked as a career coach, teaching young people how to become more successful in advancing in their careers.

Bob had never written a book before but told me he planned to write one in three months and have it published before Christmas. It was May. I laughed; I'd known many people with years of experience in writing who couldn't finish a book in that kind of time, let alone deal with all the other details of book publishing such as editing, proofreading, designing a book cover, and getting the book printed. But Bob was enthusiastic and insistent—and also planned to pay me—so I agreed to work with him.

It was a great experience. We learned from each other. I taught Bob about the art of writing and, as I read his work and talked with him, I learned about planning and project management, budgeting time, and goal setting. Bob met all his goals, completed his book, and published it by Christmas. Working with Bob was my first experience in the techniques that good coaches—whether they are sports coaches, business coaches, life coaches, or writing coaches—use to help their protégés meet their goals. Since that time I've not only read and studied more on coaching, I've worked with other coaches who also wanted to write books. As I learned from each person I worked with, my success rate in helping my clients finish their book projects also began to increase.

Writing a book is hard work. I will remind you of that often throughout this book. Writing requires time, creative energy, a sense of purpose, and a plan. It is often this last step—a plan—that writers forget. You would not hop in your car and start a road trip from Florida to California without making preparations such as researching places to stop along the way, arranging a tune-up for your car, and obtaining a roadmap or GPS to guide you. A book is no different. Before you begin to write, you must do the planning.

SMART Goals for Authors

Setting specific goals, deadlines, and rewards is one very effective way to help you keep on writing when you are discouraged. SMART is a goal-setting acronym that has been around for quite a long time with some variations. Here is mine:

S – specific
M – measurable
A – achievable
R – rewards
T - time-based

Action Items

Using SMART goals as a guide, let's set some goals for writing your book.

1. When will your manuscript be finished? Be specific. Set a date. _____

2. How will you measure your progress? Will you write daily? Weekly? How many hours will you write? How many pages at each session?

3. Is your goal achievable? Can you really write a 100,000-word manuscript in three months while writing only one hour a week? Be realistic here.

4. How will you reward yourself when you reach your milestones?

5. Make sure your goal is timely. "I'm going to write a book in the next ten months, not the next ten years."

Number Four in my SMART goal list is rewards. Finishing and publishing your book is, of course, the final big reward, but writing your book is a long process so giving yourself small rewards as you meet certain goals can help you to stay on track.

Rewarding good behavior works for kids so why shouldn't it work for you? Set small rewards for small goals, a relaxing cup of tea for finishing 1,000 words, for example. Set larger rewards for larger goals—a night of fun with your favorite video, popcorn, and maybe some friends to share it—for completing a chapter. And don't forget to set a really nice reward for actually finishing your book!

Chapter 5
Put Yourself Out There

Tears are words that need to be written.
— *Paulo Coelho*

When you publish a book you make yourself vulnerable. You are putting your thoughts and ideas out there for everyone to see and to judge. It doesn't matter whether you are writing fiction or nonfiction, a romance, sci-fi, or even a business book. The act of publishing says, "I have something so important that I think others can benefit from reading about it." And that's a scary proposition.

When I wrote my first book on writing, I felt incredibly exposed. How could I, who had never worked for a Big Six publishing company, dare to give advice on publishing? I was sure everyone would see me as a fraud. Talk about impostor syndrome! I was a classic example.

I had been publishing for years as a journalist, and my byline was on articles for newspapers and magazines in several states. I'd even owned a small, local magazine for a while. I had helped more than a dozen authors successfully publish books by that time, yet I still felt shy, embarrassed, vulnerable—the list of adjectives can go on and on.

Luckily, I had good friends and a great business coach who convinced me that not only could I write a book, but I needed to write it. And writing for newspapers and magazines had helped thicken my skin. Everyone makes mistakes in their job. But only journalists put their name on an article for everyone they know in town to read and to see if a mistake is made. And yes, I made my share of them.

My funniest story on dealing with mistakes is the day I took a call at my desk at the *Butler Eagle* and the woman on the other end of the phone said, "I'm having a really bad day, and I just need to complain to someone about something." She went on to tell me that one of the words in a boldface subheading had been syllabicated incorrectly. I apologized for the mistake (it had been mine, by the way, but that was mere coincidence) and told her I hoped her day got better. It was easy to laugh off that call, but at other times it was not so easy to laugh off criticism.

This is my roundabout way of telling you that if you are worried about making yourself vulnerable by writing a book, you are not alone. Any book you write is the product of your mind and heart. It is your baby, and you are putting it out into the cold cruel world to see if people like it.

The most vulnerable type of writing you can do is memoir. You are putting the events of your life and your very personal feelings about those events on display for the world. It's difficult. Writing a memoir is one of the most courageous acts anyone can do. I always said I'd never write my memoir unless I was the last man standing—the only surviving family member. I didn't wait quite that long, but my fear of offending family members, having them disagree with my interpretation of events, or just thinking that what I had written was silly or stupid held me back even as I started writing my book.

The first piece of advice I can give you to help you get over this fear is the Nike slogan: *Just do it.* If you don't start, you'll never know if you can finish. And if you don't show your work to someone—whether it is a friend, family member, or an editor—you'll never know if what you have written resonates with others.

The second piece of advice is: *Don't apologize.* Before publishing my memoir I gave it to a couple of family members to look over. My son's first comment surprised me: "Don't keep telling us this is only your opinion and other people might remember things differently. You make us lose faith in your voice as the narrator."

At first I wanted to tell him he was wrong. It felt very important to me to explain that other people might remember events differently. Then I realized he was absolutely right. And I was torn between patting myself on the back for raising such a smart son and being irritated because he was correct.

This is your memoir. It's your interpretation of events. If

the other people involved in your life want to interpret it differently, let them write their own book!

In working with people who are writing memoirs, I've found they are often worried about what family members or good friends who are portrayed in their book will think about what is said about them. They envision loved ones not speaking to them, yelling at them, banning them from Thanksgiving dinner, and more. What I've discovered is that the biggest complaint my authors tell me from their relatives and friends is that they were not mentioned enough. "You didn't write about this event. You didn't tell enough about that." In other words, "you didn't say enough about me." Once again, just tell them to go write their own book.

Maybe you have a kind, loving, and supportive family. Maybe you have no difficult family dynamics to negotiate. Maybe they will be proud of you for writing your memoir. Or maybe you will be banned from Thanksgiving dinner. It doesn't matter. You'll still worry. It's only natural. But once again, the only way to find out is to write and publish your book.

Action Item

Write down your fears about publishing your memoir, then look at them honestly. In my experience, most family members and friends of authors react favorably to their work. And if they don't, well, you just need to tell them to get over it.

Chapter 6
Hybrid Memoir & Memoir Plus

Tell the story of the mountains you climbed. Your words could become a page in someone else's survival guide.
— Morgan Harper Nichols

Hybrid Memoir

As noted in Chapter 1, hybrid memoir is a combination of memoir and one or more additional genres, such as how-to, inspirational, historical fiction, or poetry.

Most memoirs—with the exception of a few celebrity books—fall into the hybrid or memoir plus category. A memoir, as opposed to autobiography, has a message, a "lesson learned." This message may be as obvious as how to accomplish something or how to overcome a specific challenge. Or it can be more subtle, as in books that combine memoir and an inspirational message.

Understanding that you are writing a hybrid book can help you think about exactly what you want to say and how to say it.

The term "memoir plus" was coined by writer Leigh Stein to categorize books that are more than just a straight narrative of someone's life. The point of memoir plus and hybrid memoir is that the reader learns something in addition to just hearing a story about the writer's life.

Most readers don't usually type in "memoir" as a keyword when searching for a book online or look for the "memoir" section in the bookstore. Online, that word is too broad, and most bookstores only have a tiny section dedicated to memoir, if there is one at all.

So how will readers find your memoir? They will search for it by subject or theme. You might think I have skipped far ahead from planning your book to marketing your book, but I have not. If you understand right from the start that you are writing a book not just about you but also one that has a specific message that readers are looking for, it will help you plan and write your book.

Kesha Cox, an author I worked with on her memoir, *Never Settle for Less*, discusses the problems she had in school after being labeled "slow," at a time when the term "dyslexia" was just becoming known. She is also a minister's wife, and her story is faith-based. While essentially a memoir, her message of overcoming challenges through faith in God means that readers looking for a book about either overcoming learning disabilities or a book on the Christian faith would find it interesting.

Kesha's book is told in a linear fashion. Another author I have worked with, Sherri A. Lynn, uses a different method to write her books. Sherri is working on her third hybrid memoir. In each book she had a different theme. Her first book, *All My Heroes Have Fur, Fins & Feathers*, discusses her work as an animal communicator and healer, and how she came to understand and develop her abilities with animals. Each chapter in the book is a separate story and tells of an encounter with a different animal. Each story has its own message within the larger theme of the entire work.

In her second book, *Unraveled, From Sibling Abuse to Sacred Self,* Sherri discusses her childhood abuse at the hands of her sibling and how it has affected the rest of her life and relationships. Again, she does not tell her story in a linear way. In her first chapter we learn about her mother's death, and it is only in later chapters that we learn in more detail about her childhood. While it sounds as if the book skips around in a random fashion, it does not. It is organized in a way that shows her growing understanding of how early childhood incidents have shaped the rest of her life—and how coming to terms with these incidents has helped her learn and grow as a person.

Most successful memoirs that are written for a larger audience than just family members are actually hybrid works. Before you begin to write, think about what message you want your audience to take away and remember when they close the last page of your book.

Action Items

Here are some questions to ask yourself before starting your memoir.
- What knowledge would I like my readers to gain from reading my book?
- What do I want them to think or feel?
- What actions would I like them to take after reading my book?

Chapter 7
The Arc of Change

If there were only one truth, you couldn't paint a hundred canvases on the same theme.
— *Pablo Picasso*

Every book—whether it is fiction or nonfiction, memoir or how-to—needs an arc of change. That is a fancy way of saying that you are taking the reader on a journey from where you start to where you are at the end of the book.

The change can be physical, mental, or emotional. Even if you are writing a straight, linear biography, showing a change in how you develop from child to successful adult is a necessary part of your story. If your life is static, if nothing that happens affects you or changes you, you're a pretty boring person. And if you were really that boring, you would have no desire to write about your life.

So what is the change you want to tell your readers about?

- Have you discovered the secret of success and made a million dollars?
- Have you conquered a disease?
- Have you overcome a difficult childhood?
- Have you won an Olympic medal?

These all sound like extraordinary topics. After looking at this list, you might say to yourself, "I've done nothing that important." But you have. You've had an "aha" moment. It can be great or small, it can have come all at once or over a period of years. Understanding the change you want to tell us about is an important first step in organizing your story. In memoir the arc of change in your life is the theme of your book.

Remember those high school English classes when you had to write compositions on the theme of exciting books such as *Billy Budd* or *The Crucible*? No one could have hated writing those essays as much as I did. Maybe that's why it took me years to admit that all writing—no matter how short or how long—must have a theme or purpose. If you don't have a purpose, why write at all? Once I learned this lesson, I became a better writer.

A Confession

When I first began writing my memoir I did not have a theme. I had a collection of six or seven slightly related short stories and no idea what to do next. I'd totally forgotten everything I taught others to do in writing. That's when I showed the stories to a writer friend who told me: "These are great. They are fun stories. But what are you trying to tell us? What holds all these stories together?"

It was my own personal aha moment. I realized I'd never given a thought to the endgame when I started writing my book.

Sometimes writing doesn't follow a straight path. It took me a couple of months, several false starts, and a lot of soul searching to decide what arc of change I wanted to tell about in my memoir.

Writing intuitively is an important part of becoming an author, particularly when writing something as personal as a memoir. Just because you have developed an outline doesn't mean that you should shut down this intuition. As you go through the process of writing your book, you will think about or remember details that you want to add. A combination of planning and intuition can help you create the best story.

Action Items

To find your theme ask yourself these questions:
- What was your "aha" moment?
- How did this moment affect and change you?
- What lesson did you learn that you want your readers to understand?

Now write down the theme or arc of change that you want to express in your memoir.

The first time you write the theme for your book it might take you a paragraph or even two. That's an excellent place to start, but if it has taken you that many words to describe your theme, you are either not clear about your purpose or you are attempting to include too many themes or purposes in your book. I call this the "everything including the kitchen sink syndrome" in book writing.

Take a look at your paragraph and try to condense it. If you are having trouble, ask a friend to look it over and help you refine it. Rewrite it, cutting out any ideas that are not essential. Don't stop until you can state your theme in one to two sentences.

Chapter 8
Organize Your Book

Organizing is a journey, not a destination.
— *Author Unknown*

Finding your theme is probably the hardest part of writing a book. Now that you have discovered it, I know that you want to get started on writing your first chapter. However, you still have some organizational work to do. Your next step is to create an outline. Don't panic! I don't mean those formal outlines you were taught back in high school English class with Roman numerals and capital letters, although I must admit that's the type of outline I prefer. You can make your outline in any way that feels comfortable to you. You won't be graded on this outline, and no one else—except possibly your editor or writing coach—needs to see it. If you make your outline now, you'll have a lot easier time writing your memoir than I did.

I know several writers who use a "mind map" (a graphic way to diagram your book). Other writers' "outlines" are made on Post-it® notes or index cards with one topic or idea written on each. They lay out the cards on a large surface, then arrange and rearrange them until the order feels right. Another author took this idea to the next level. She painted her walls with dry erase paint, which turns a wall into a giant whiteboard. She can now scribble her ideas all over the walls of her room.

It doesn't matter what method you use to organize your book, but you do need to decide how many chapters you will have and what basic information will go in each chapter.

In addition to your overall theme, each chapter should also have its own mini-theme or purpose that works to enhance and move the reader forward in understanding the overall thesis of your book.

Your outline is an organizational and memory aid only. Spend only enough time on it so that in a couple of weeks or months when you are ready to write Chapter 6 you don't need to spend a lot of time figuring out exactly what you had planned to write about. Taking some time now to outline your book will make writing it go faster later on. Don't spend a lot of time perfecting the grammar and style of your outline. One writer may need only a few words or phrases to remember what is planned for each chapter. Another may prefer to write full sentences or paragraphs. I know many authors who believe strongly in the "seat of the pants" style of writing. I've tried both. If you are a "pantser," go for it. But if, like me, you're more comfortable with a roadmap when you start out on an adventure, here are some suggestions to get you started.

Action Item

- Include your title, theme, and a short summary for each of your chapters in your outline.
- Make some notes on your introduction. However, I've noticed that most people who write the introduction first go back and rewrite their introduction after they have finished their book.
- Once you have taken these steps, you are almost ready to start writing your book.

Chapter 9
Who Is Your Reader?

The aim of marketing is to know and understand the customer so well the product or service fits him and sells itself.
— Peter Drucker

If you've spent any time at all in business, you've heard the phrase, "find your target market." As a writer, your target market is your reader. When I ask the writers I work with who their target reader is, the most common answer I get is "everyone," or some variation of the word such as "every parent" or "everyone in business" or "everyone who likes to cook" or "everyone who reads mysteries" or another answer equally as broad.

Some people try to narrow it down a bit. "My audience is women" (okay, you've narrowed it to half the population) or "my audience is women between the ages of thirty and sixty" (now we've got it to one quarter of the population). All these answers are still too expansive to define your true target reader.

Before you begin to write your book, come up with as detailed a description of your target reader as possible. The more you know about your readers, the better equipped you will be in writing a book they will be interested in buying and reading. This is particularly true when writing a memoir. Is your target reader your family? Or is it a more general audience?

Are your audience experts on your subject or are they beginners in the field? In memoir your "experts" might be your family and friends who know all about you and your history. If they are your target market, you might not have to explain in detail certain family relationships or other family history. But knowing the answer to your target reader is about more than just having a background knowledge of you and your family. As I noted the previous chapter, your book needs a theme. Is it overcoming cancer? Then you must assume your audience does not know all the medical terms that you learned on your journey. Is it how you developed the best widget and became a business success? Assume your reader is not familiar with the ins and outs of business and is reading your memoir to learn how you became successful and to follow in your footsteps. Knowing who your reader is will help you adjust your vocabulary to the correct level. A book written for beginners that does not explain complex vocabulary specific to your subject will quickly turn off readers who are unfamiliar but want to learn.

    I often suggest writers think of a specific person who would enjoy reading their books. As you write keep this person in mind. How would this person react to what you have written? Would the person understand the explanation or description you just wrote or be bored and find it too elementary? Would your reader chuckle or gasp in horror at the right places?

Action Items

Knowing who your reader is has a huge impact on how you write your book. Here are a few questions to ask yourself about your target readers.

- What is their gender? The target reader for my memoir, *Hibiscus Strong*, is women who enjoy stories about quirky Southern characters, along with Florida history buff.
- What is their age? Most memoir readers are middle-aged and above.
- What is their income level? This can vary depending on the specific theme of your book.
- What are their hobbies?
- What other books do they read?
- How much do they know about the subject of your book?

Write a description of your target reader. This person can be someone you know or a fictionalized, composite character. Either way, make your description as detailed as you can. When you work on your book, picture this person sitting at the table across from you. Write as if you are having a conversation with them.

Chapter 10
Dialogue and Point of View

*Don't tell me the moon is shining;
show me the glint of light on broken glass.*
— *Anton Chekhov*

Should your memoir include dialogue? Yes! Does it matter that you don't remember exactly what was said in a particular conversation? Or that you are relating a conversation you have been told about but were not present for? Yes, again. And no, these statements do not contradict each other.

A memoir—even a hybrid memoir that is, in part, a how-to book—differs from many other types of nonfiction books in that it has the element of storytelling. You are writing *creative nonfiction,* which is a factual story told in a narrative way.

Show Me, Don't Tell Me

When many people start writing a memoir, they begin by just narrating the facts. And yes, you do need some narration in your memoir just as you need some dialogue. A work that is all dialogue is a play. A work that is all narration is just boring. You need a balance of the two to keep the story flowing and make your reader want to continue reading to the end.

I'm using a short passage from a privately published memoir here to illustrate my point. It was written by a now-deceased friend of my mother and was not published. I've removed any identifying information—particularly because I'm using her writing as a poor example.

"While Daddy was in Chicago Mother and I lived with my grandmother…in her little house…in Grand Rapids. I came to love that house and "Baba" as I called her. Some of my earliest memories are of the pink rambling roses on the front *porch and the long, long driveway beneath tall trees back to the garage. ...my cousins,...sons of my mother's sister, used to join me in raiding the rhubarb bed and chewing it on the spot."*

The book continues to tell us how much she enjoyed warm rhubarb pie and her grandmother's chicken and biscuits. But imagine if she had instead given us a miniature vignette here, complete with dialogue, of the three cousins in the garden picking the rhubarb. Did they have to sneak in because they would get in trouble if caught? Was Grandma saving the rhubarb for a special occasion? What did it taste like? Crunchy? Sweet? Tart? All the above? (I'm not a rhubarb fan myself and have only eaten under protest a few times so I'm guessing here.) At any rate you get my point. The author *told us* about eating rhubarb from her grandmother's garden. She didn't *show us* why this is such a fond memory for her.

Memoir, like any other story, needs a combination of both narration and dialogue. Narration moves the story along, sets the scene, and lets the reader know what someone is thinking. Dialogue *shows* us what is happening, what other characters are thinking and feeling, and helps us understand any conflict and resolution between characters. And yes, I know we are writing about real people here, but when they are on the page, they are your characters—even when one of them is you.

Discussing dialogue brings us to dialect. Do different people in your book have particular speech patterns? Catch phrases they often use? Accents? It can be difficult to portray these differences, particularly for characters that do not speak in the same way you do. If most of your characters are Northerners, for example, but one is from the South, do they "y'all" frequently? Teenagers often use slang. And different ethnic groups have different ways of phrasing what they mean.

Point of View

From what point of view are you telling your story? Obviously, it is from your own perspective, but there is much more to it than that. And different parts of your story may call for different points of view.

Point of view sets the tone of the story. You may remember from your English grammar classes about the three points of view: first person, second person, and third person. But when you begin to write you'll find out there are more.

First person: The narrator tells the story from their own point of view, using "I" or "me" to narrate the story. First person is particularly suited to memoir because you are obviously telling your own story. But using first person throughout a long book can be limiting. When using first person, all your ideas and observations are shown only through what you, the narrator, knows. You cannot know exactly what another person is thinking unless they tell you. You can speculate, but you are limited in showing that second character's thoughts and emotions.

Second person: This point of view is a little used technique in fiction because it is difficult to sustain. Using second person can enhance the reader's feeling of being part of the story. "You crack your eyes open slowly, blinking at the bright sunshine streaming in through the curtains. It is Saturday. No school! You jump out of bed and hurry to get dressed." While interesting, it is not only inappropriate for most memoirs but is also quite difficult to sustain.

However, in hybrid memoir—particularly memoir that includes a "how-to" component—using second person can be a very effective way to draw your reader in and make them feel that they can accomplish what you are explaining to them.

Third person: When using third person the writer tells the story as if they are not part of the story, using "he, "she," or "they"—even when describing incidents or actions that they themselves are involved in. Third person has its place in memoir. You may want to describe events that you have been told but did not personally witness; for example, this approach works when another character has described the events to you.

To confuse matters even further, third person narration is broken into three types: omniscient, limited or dramatic, and objective.

Third person omniscient: This is probably the point of

view we are most familiar with as readers. Many novels use it, and as writers it is wonderful to be that all-knowing, all-seeing overlord who not only makes all the characters do what you want them to do but understands completely their motivations for doing so. Unfortunately, in real life this is not the case, and so it may not be appropriate for your memoir. While we know our own motivations for our actions, we don't always know why everyone around us is making certain decisions or acting in certain ways.

Third person limited or third person dramatic: In this point of view, the narrator uses "he," "she," or "they" throughout the book but is only allowed to see into the thoughts of one character. The narrator, and therefore the reader, only knows and understands the motivations and emotions of one character in the story. It can be quite tempting for the writer to slip from dramatic to omniscient narration. If you choose to use this point of view, be very careful that you sustain it throughout the book.

Third person objective: The narrator relates the events without telling the reader the thoughts or motivations of any of the characters. This, again, can be difficult to sustain. It can make a book feel very objective. It can distance the reader from the action and also increase suspense.

You may choose to use more than one point of view in your memoir. If done well it can be very effective. If done poorly it will distract the reader.

Action Item

Here are some tips to remember when writing your memoir. Use the list to help ensure that you have been intentional in your use of point of view.

- Don't change the point of view in the middle of a sentence, a paragraph, or even a chapter without creating some kind of break to show that we have switched to a new person's viewpoint. You can create a scene break, typically three asterisks (***) centered on a separate line, to show that there is a change.
- When changing to a new point of view at the beginning of a chapter, make sure to quickly let the reader know that a new character is now taking center stage.
- Don't be haphazard when changing points of view. Make sure you know why you are changing, and be sure your reasoning makes sense.
- The best way to learn about point of view is to read widely and study the ways in which other authors use it.

Chapter 11
Your Photographs

Photographs open doors into the past, but they also allow a look into the future.
— Sally Mann

We all love our old family photographs. Whether it is a 1920s photo of our great-grandparents or last year's snapshot taken at a family picnic, we want to show them off to everyone. But is your memoir really the right place?

Of course, you say. What better place to use them? But before choosing fifty or more of your favorite photos to print in your memoir, there are some factors you need to think about.

Enhancing Your Message

The first and most important questions to ask are:

- Does the photo enhance your message?
- Does it illustrate an important point you are trying to make?
- Does it add more to the story? One picture is not always worth a thousand words.

Just using a photo because you like it, or even because it shows some of your family members, is not a good enough reason to print it in your memoir. I've spent hours trying to talk authors out of using photos that just don't make any sense with the book they are writing. "But I love this photo." "It's such a cute shot of my child/mother/spouse." Great. Take those photos, frame them, and hang them on the wall. If they don't relate to your theme, don't put them in your book. You don't need them there.

Some of us still remember the old days when a

biography, memoir, or other nonfiction book had a section in the middle of it with six or eight pages of glossy, coated paper devoted to photos. The special paper, with a gloss similar to photo paper, helped to improve the look of the photos. I have not seen this special printing technique done in years. If you are lucky enough to have a major publisher subsidizing your book, it may be possible; if not the cost of this type of printing is prohibitive.

Today photos are placed throughout the book. That means they are printed on fifty-pound white matte paper that makes good photos look mediocre, and a marginal photo will look terrible. Understanding how photos will reproduce on the printed page is important when choosing which photos you should use in your memoir.

What to Look For

Photos fade over time. Depending on the paper and ink used by the developer, as well as where the photo has been kept, fading can begin within a few months to a few years; older black and white photos can yellow, darken, or fade. If you have a good scanner, or know someone who does, some of these problems can be corrected. You'll need to scan the photos and turn them into JPEG files for use in your book. So if you have never worked with scanning photos before, take the extra step and have someone who knows about the process help you work with the photos to make them look as good as possible.

The standard for printing photos in books, magazines, and newspapers is 300 dpi or dots per inch, which refers to the number of dots of ink per inch a printer puts on the paper. In other words, if you have a really excellent scanner, it is possible to scan that original photo at 1,500 dpi, and it will look fabulous on your computer screen. But when you send your manuscript to a printer, it will be printed at 300 dpi. Most printers, including Amazon KDP and Ingram Spark, will not print at anything else. You can go to a specialty printer, and if you are only printing a few books for private distribution, you can pay the extra cost for higher quality paper and printing. But if you plan to mass produce your book, please understand that the only economically viable option is the standard printing process you will get from places such as Amazon KDP or other book printers.

So how can you tell if your photograph will reproduce well? First, realize that as you get farther away from the original print, the more problems you may have. By this I mean that you have an original photo (copy 1), which you scan onto the computer as a JPEG file (copy 2). Then you take the JPEG file and reproduce it in your book (copy 3). This third-generation copy you now have gives you even less control because it is being printed by a printing company several hundred times; each copy may have slightly more or less ink on the page. This often means that the photo in the book has more contrast than the original. The light colors get lighter, and the dark colors become darker. You begin to lose a lot of the detail in the photo.

No, this doesn't happen with every photo you reproduce in a book, but please be aware that what you see on your computer screen may look different when printed.

There are a few other factors to think about when choosing photos for your memoir.

Blurry photos: Our eyes often fill in details of images we are familiar with. For example, snapshots taken with older Kodak or Polaroid cameras may not be sharp, and strangers will just see a blurry photo because they aren't familiar with those people in your picture.

Composition: Look at the entire photo. Our eyes tend to ignore the telephone lines and electric wires that crisscross the photo of our childhood home. But again, strangers will see the lines, not the house. And that picture of you and your family with the entire range of Smoky Mountains in the background may be a great memory, but if the people are just tiny specks, it is not going to enhance your book.

I have a photo I love of me with my husband in college. It's black and white, and we are standing in front of someone's dorm desk. On top of the desk is a snake plant, and its leaves seem to growing straight out of my head. Someday I'm going to scan it and photoshop out those pesky leaves, but somehow I've never gotten around to it. Photos flatten perspective. That plant, which was a few feet away, appears to be on top of my head in the photo. Look at the trees, telephone poles, and other objects in the background. With a little editing many problems can be fixed. If they can't consider not using that particular photo in your memoir.

Action Item

Ask an objective person—one who is not a family member or friend—to help you with this exercise.

- Collect the photos you are considering using in your book. Sort them into similar shots, then decide which one is the best. You don't need five pictures of Uncle Vinnie, even *if* he was your favorite relative. You only need one.
- Look carefully at the photos you have chosen. Are they sharp and clear? Is there good contrast? And most important, does the photo help tell your story?

Chapter 12
Copyright and Disclaimers

The acorn of fact is usually the progenitor of the oak, which when full grown no longer has any resemblance to the acorn.
— April 29, 1954, Harry Ander for Joseph A. Maggio, complainant; Horace S. Manges for Charles Scribner's Sons, defendant; and Myles J. Lane for Columbia Pictures Corporation, defendant

Intellectual property is complex. My first disclaimer when discussing these issues is that I am not a lawyer. If you have questions about any documents or photos that you want to use in your memoir, please consult an attorney. Just because you happen to have a paper copy of a document or photograph may not mean that you have the right to print it in your book.

Copyright gives the creator of the image the ability to financially benefit from the work—even after the creator's death. Family snapshots may have copyright protection, even if they have never been published. Image copyrights last for the duration of an image creator's life plus seventy years. In some cases, if the image is registered with the U.S. Copyright Office before it expires, it may be eligible for more years of protection.

Public Domain

If a photograph, document, or literary work is in the public domain, it means it is not eligible for copyright protection, or that protection has expired. No permission is needed to copy or use works that are in the public domain. Public domain works can serve as the foundation for new creative works and can be quoted extensively.

As of January 1, 2022, the original "Winnie the Pooh" book written by A.A. Milne entered the public domain. In 2023 a British independent filmmaker released *Winnie-the-Pooh: Blood and Honey,* a slasher film about the beloved bear. As sad as it might seem, it was perfectly legal.

Stock Images

"Stock image" is a broad term for photos, graphics, and even short animations licensed by the creator for commercial use. A few good websites to look for stock images are shutterstock.com, 123rf.com, and for historical photos, Gettyimages.com. Do not grab an image off a website and use it in your book, on your website, or on social media without checking if it is in the public domain or if it is a stock photo or if a specific creator owns the rights. Using stock photos without a license can result in fines, lawsuits, or having your work removed from Amazon KDP and other bookselling sites.

Getty Images, which owns thousands of the most famous historical photographs, is particularly known for policing its work. Do not assume that because you have often seen a well-known historical image that it is in the public domain. Getty, Time-Life, and other news organizations hold the copyright to many of these photographs. Always check before using something.

A Chance Encounter

One day in about 1998 I was walking through my local Target store looking for cat litter. I happened to be in the home goods section, standing near the framed artwork that people buy to decorate their homes. I looked up and saw my Uncle Ed. Not my actual uncle; he had died 20 years before. I saw his photograph. In Target. In fact, I saw a half dozen of the photos in a rack for sale.

I knew it was my uncle. My aunt had this same photo framed on her wall. My uncle is sitting in a speedboat waving at the camera. I saw it every time I visited her home. The picture was obviously a copy of the same photo. But how had it come to be in Target?

My uncle had raced speedboats back in the 1940s and

'50s and was sponsored by the well-known boat manufacturer, Chris-Craft. The photo was one of a series taken for publicity. Chris-Craft owned the rights to the photos, and after doing some research I discovered they had donated some pictures to a maritime museum. The museum then licensed them as a way to raise funds. Yes, I have an original hard copy of the photograph. And no, I do not own the copyright. I will not be reproducing that particular photo in my memoir or on my blog about Miami history.

This is a very short discussion of a very complex issue. Once again, if you have questions please consult an attorney who is an expert in copyright law.

Copyright infringement is a major issue for authors, photographers, graphic artists, and others in creative fields. You do not want your words to be stolen and used by someone else. Please respect other artists, and make sure you are not infringing on their intellectual property rights.

Music

It seems like a no-brainer to write the lyrics to a song that is important to your life in your memoir. But please, don't be hasty. The rules for using lyrics are even more strict than the rules for quoting written works. Lawyers, editors, and proofreaders that I trust all caution against it because of the complexity. In looking up information about copyright laws for music and lyrics, the best advice I found came from NOLO.com, a website with a mission is to "help consumers and small businesses find answers to their everyday legal and business questions." The answer on the website follows all the other advice I've heard and states: "Unfortunately, there are no fixed standards as to how much of a song you can use without infringing the song owner's copyright."

My best advice on quoting lyrics is: ***Just don't.***

Disclaimers

I suggest you always add at least a very basic disclaimer on your book's copyright page. Here is an example:

"No part of this book may be used or reproduced in any manner whatsoever without the written permission of the author, except in the case of brief quotations embodied in critical articles and reviews."

Disclaimers are a way of protecting the author. Do they assure you will not be sued? No. But they do help to protect you. In memoir a disclaimer offers transparency from the author, essentially spelling out that "these are my memories, and other people may have different opinions."

These types of statements can reduce the risk of liability, such as a disclaimer saying that while the author is discussing medical issues, the reader must consult a doctor before following any advice. They can make it clear if you have changed the names of real people to protect the innocent—or the guilty. Disclaimers can help establish your expertise as well as state that you may have made errors or omissions in your writing. Don't discount the use of disclaimers on your copyright page, and do make them as extensive as you think necessary.

Trigger Warnings

Warnings about content that may upset a reader are becoming more and more common in both fiction and nonfiction. Does your book have explicit language? Does it have graphic scenes of death, rape, abuse, or other violence?

Don't be offended by the need to put this type of disclaimer in your book. A trigger warning is a polite way for an author to warn a reader that they might be offended or upset by some content in the book.

Registering Your Copyright

The registration process with the U.S. Copyright Office is much simpler than most government procedures, and one you can easily do yourself. However, you should seek professional advice from an attorney who specializes in intellectual property law if you have any complex questions or problems with copyright.

According to the U.S. Copyright Office, "Copyright is a

form of protection provided by the laws of the United States (title 17, U.S. Code) to the authors of 'original works of authorship,' including literary, dramatic, musical, artistic, and certain other intellectual works. This protection is available to both published and unpublished works."

Copyright exists from the moment a work is created, and registration is voluntary. In other words, it is not necessary for you to register your work with the U.S. Copyright Office for it to be protected. However, there are benefits in registering a work. First and foremost, you must have registered your work if you wish to bring a lawsuit for infringement.

You do not need a lawyer to register your work with the U.S. Copyright Office. All you need to do is go to www.copyright.gov, fill out an application form, and pay a small fee.

Let me repeat this one more time: If you have any questions about intellectual property rights or copyright, consult an attorney who specializes in this area.

Action Items

- Go over your book with an eye toward copyright protection. Have you used anything you have questions about? If so, check with an expert.
- Check your copyright page. Make sure you the copyright symbol (©), your name, and the year are prominently displayed. For example: Copyright © 2024 by Karen Hodges Miller.

Chapter 13
What Comes Next?

Publishing a book is like stuffing a note into a bottle and hurling it into the sea. Some bottles drown, some come safe to land, where the notes are read and then possibly cherished, or else misinterpreted, or else understood all too well by those who hate the message
You never know who your readers might be.
— *Margaret Atwood*

You've spent weeks and months—maybe even years—writing, editing, and rewriting, and now you finally have a completed manuscript. It's as shiny as a polished apple, and you can't wait to share it with the world. How do you get your work from a computer document to a professional-looking format, the book you've dreamed of publishing?

These days you have a lot of options to choose from in the publishing world and many decisions to make. Should you publish your work as a traditional paper book, an e-book, or both? Should you look for an agent and try to sell your manuscript to a large publishing house, go the do-it-yourself route, or find something in between?

Unless you are already famous or have a unique story to tell, the best way to get your story from a manuscript onto Amazon is to self-publish.

Three terms you hear these days that have changed the face of the publishing industry are digital printing, print-on-demand (or POD), and e-books.

- **Digital printing** is a process in which books or other materials are stored as computer files and printed on laser printers. The advantages for printers, publishers, and authors are many. For printers, less storage space for old files and less setup time (among other factors) have substantially reduced the cost of printing books. This means more printing companies can now get into the game and print good-quality books in small quantities. For authors and publishers, faster turnaround times and lower setup fees make it economically feasible to produce a small number of books at one time. Books written for small niche audiences have a much greater chance of economic success than they had in the past. Digital printing is called "print on demand," but there is also a second definition for POD.

- ***POD*** is a business model in which books are printed only as they are needed. If an author is planning a seminar and expects to sell fifty books, they can order exactly that many at one time. If they think they can sell seventy books, they can order that amount. At the other end of the selling spectrum, if a book is listed on a book website, such as Amazon, an individual reader can order one book, which will be individually printed and delivered to them.

- ***E-books.*** I'm constantly amazed at how many authors I speak with who are sure they want to have their book published in this way but have never actually read or even looked at an e-book, or who don't understand the differences between formatting a paper book and formatting an e-book. The broadest definition of an e-book is a book that can be downloaded and read on an electronic device. A PDF can be considered an e-book, and many people do sell or give away books in PDF form on their websites, and a PDF can also be read on an e-reader.

In addition to new printing techniques, the internet has also dramatically changed the way in which books are distributed. No longer must the author lug books from store to store like an old-fashioned door-to-door sales representative. These days authors can go right to the reader through book websites or through their personal or business website. With Amazon's KDP publishing program, you can publish a book at practically no cost.

Self-Publishing vs. Do-It-Yourself

There is a difference between self-publishing and what I call "do-it-yourself" publishing. The do-it-yourself author tries to handle every aspect of book publishing from writing to editing to cover design to book marketing in the cheapest way possible. Don't get me wrong; I'm all for being frugal. To get readers and make money in today's competitive book market, an author can't do it all.

To be successful, you must realize you, the author, are now a business owner. You have two products to sell: your book and yourself. Before you decide whether to self-publish or begin the search for a publisher, you have several aspects to consider.

Independent Publishers

Today authors are no longer stuck with only two choices: the search for an agent and giant publishing house to pick up your book or the do-it-yourself method. There are several basic models for publishing: traditional, do-it-yourself, small independent publishers, and hybrid models.

Assisted self-publishers, or hybrid publishers, have many different models for payment. One model is a "buy-in" in which the author guarantees to purchase a certain number of books. In another model the publisher asks the author to pay for the production, marketing, and other services in a package or on an a la carte basis.

Small independent publishers often look for authors who are writing for niche markets. These books may not become the next national blockbuster, but they do have a market.

Let me stress there is no one right way to publish. I've heard of people who were happy with each type of publisher, and I've also heard horror stories from authors who have used each type of publisher. Do your research, not just about the type of publishing you choose but the individual company within that group. That is the best way to ensure that you will have a good outcome and be happy with the services you receive and with the final product—your book.

There are now ads on television and the internet from publishers offering to publish your book. Look at their contracts carefully. What are they offering you? What are their charges? If they tell you they can make you a bestseller even before looking at your manuscript, run. No one can guarantee that.

Action Items

What type of publisher are you interested in? If you have not yet decided, now is the time to do the research.

- Go online and do Google searches for independent publishers, traditional publishers, and publishing agents.
- Gather their contact information as well as other basic information about each one. Then start contacting them.

You'll never know if you can get a publishing deal unless you try!

Chapter 14
Decisions, Decisions

May your choices reflect your hopes, not your fears.
— *Nelson Mandela*

If you are an expert in graphic arts, editing, proofreading, formatting the interior pages, e-book formatting, indexing, marketing, sales, and book distribution, then go ahead and do it all yourself. Not an expert in all these areas? Don't have the time or the desire to become an expert? Then look for someone to help with these services. You can find a full-service publisher or consultant or look for individuals who can help with what is needed.

Here is a list of items or tasks necessary to publish a book that looks and reads both polished and professional.

- Editing
- Formatting as a paper book, e-book, or both
- Proofreading
- Cover design
- Obtaining an International Standard Book Number (ISBN)
- Uploading your book to Amazon and other websites
- Distribution
- Marketing

Your Creative Team

Who should be on your team? Authors often start with the people they know, family members or friends they respect. Ask them to read the manuscript and give their reactions to it. This can be a great place to start, but when it comes to developing a creative team, it is not where an author should end.

Family and friends can offer good advice; when writing a memoir they may be either a help or a hindrance. But in addition to their closeness to the subject of the work, if they are not professional editors, proofreaders, graphic artists, marketers, publicists, or publishers, they cannot really offer you the best, most professional advice about your book. I often hear people say such comments as "My mother is a teacher; she's excellent at grammar so I had her edit my book." Or "My best friend is a really good artist so they drew my cover for me." I've even had one author call me that she wanted to make a change in her cover design based on advice from her cat sitter.

Yes, you do need someone to check over your grammar and illustrate the cover, but that's not all that is needed. Who else will make a good addition to the book's creative team?

Editor: A traditional or independent publisher may assign an editor. When self-publishing a professional editor is a must. Yes, your best friend may be a really great writer, a teacher, or an expert blogger, but more than that is needed. You need an editor to read your book and flag the following details.

- Missing or incomplete information
- Grammar and spelling errors
- Marketability of the work
- Consistent and appropriate style applying guidelines such as *The Chicago Manual of Style* or *The Associated Press Stylebook*
- Ease of reading and a style appropriate to the audience

I've used the word "style" twice in my list, each time to mean something different. On the one hand, "style" refers to the consistency of content such as the use of numerals versus written numbers and italics versus quotation marks for referring to books and periodicals. If not consistent, such details are subtle signs that say "unprofessional" to the reader—sometimes without their even realizing it. In the corporate world the term "best practices" is used to describe this need.

Several style manuals are available. *The Chicago Manual of Style* is used most often by both fiction and nonfiction writers. While writers with a journalistic background may be most familiar with *The Associated Press Stylebook* (also referred to as AP style), it is not used often outside of journalistic works. Scholarly works in the social or behavioral sciences often require the *Publication Manual of the American Psychological Association* (also referred to as APA style). Other professions also have style manuals. Make sure to use the manual most appropriate for your book's subject or genre.

There is another meaning for the word "style." It also refers to the tone in which a book is written. For example, a book aimed at an academic audience will have a very different style or tone than one written for the mass market. Before asking someone to read your work, make sure that person understands the target market and the style of writing that is most appropriate.

Formatting expert: Many details are involved in formatting a book, from choosing the page size and margin size to correctly placing the headers and footers. If you plan on publishing both a paper version and an e-book, two separate files are needed, one for each. I recommend creating the file for your paper book first, send it to a proofreader, then create the e-book file from that version. There are a number of details, along with a few tricks, to be aware of when formatting your book. I discuss them in greater detail in my book *Self-Publishing: You Can Do This! What You Need to Know to Write, Publish & Market Your Book*.

Proofreader or line editor: Once your book is formatted, it should go to an excellent proofreader. Good proofreaders are hard to find. They have an eye for detail and a knowledge of grammar and style. A good proofreader is one of the biggest differences between producing a book that is professional and one that reads as if it was written by an amateur.

Cover designer: While many people have artistic friends who offer to create a cover illustration, you will need a professional graphic artist to develop the front cover, back cover, and spine. This person should be an expert in a graphics software program such as Adobe Illustrator, as well as Adobe Acrobat. A book cover is much more than just a great illustration. It is a combination of graphics and text that is compelling enough to make a potential reader want to pick up your book in a bookstore or click on it on a website and purchase it. A book cover is the first impression a target reader has of your book. Studies have shown viewers look at a website for ten to twenty seconds when choosing whether to continue to view it or to move on. Your book cover is one small fraction of an Amazon page or other website so assume a potential reader will look at the cover for just a fraction of that time. This means a book cover must be attractive and professional and must stand out enough to attract a reader in less than ten seconds.

Marketer: You should consult with a marketing professional about your website, use of social media, and other ways you can get the word out about your book. A professional marketing company can help plan events or seminars, develop flyers or postcards promoting your book, and work with you to develop an overall marketing plan.

Publicist: Public relations (PR) is a complex field with many nuances so before we can discuss finding the right publicist for you, here are a few quick definitions: Public relations is the art of developing a strategic message, and publicity is the act of getting your message out through the best channels.

If you decide to hire a publicist to help promote your book and yourself as an expert in your field, make sure to hire someone with a reputation for working successfully with authors. The fine art of public relations is very specialized. A PR person who has worked with local small business owners, for example, may not have the contacts needed to get bookings on radio or television talk shows appropriate for your topic. A marketer and publicist should be able to work together to promote you and your book. The best way to find a book publicist is to go online and search. Read several websites, then call and talk with three or four agents before you make your choice.

Too Many Cooks

The last few months before a book is finally published and available to the public can be both exciting and hectic. Because first-time authors have never published a book before, they may feel unsure about every decision that is made—no matter how large or small. I've seen that even after choosing a creative team they respect, like, and trust, many authors give in to the temptation to ask everyone they know for an opinion on every aspect of the book. I'm not talking about making appropriate corrections to the final galley proof. I'm talking about attempting to make last-minute major changes in the concept of the book, its design, or its pricing.

If you've ever sat over coffee with a group of friends and discussed any subject, no matter how important or trivial, you will have noticed for each person at the table there often seems to be at least two opinions—usually conflicting.

Action Items

List the types of experts you need: editor, graphic artist, marketing. Do you already know experts in these areas? If not, where can you find people to help you?

One great resource is the Independent Book Publishers Association (IBPA) online directory of independent contractors. You can find out more about the organization in the resources section of this book.

Chapter 15
Beta Readers and Advance Readers

A beta reader is a person who reads a book, typically without payment, before it is published to check for errors or plot holes and to make suggestions for improvement.

An advance reader receives an early, final copy of the book and is asked to write a review.

I never used beta readers in the past; I have always used a paid developmental editor, sometimes two, and a proofreader. Then I started hearing a lot of writer friends talk about using beta readers. Their experiences seemed to be mostly positive so when writing my memoir, I decided to use additional beta readers to give me feedback. Why? Because even after my developmental editor had taken apart my book and put it back together again differently, I was unsure if my theme was coming through.

My first beta reader was my niece. I made a few mistakes in choosing her. First, she has four-year-old twins so her time to sit and concentrate on reading is limited. Second, she loves me and was totally uncritical. She thought everything I sent her was wonderful—even when I knew it wasn't.

Next, I asked a few writer friends to read the book. One finished it quickly and gave me excellent feedback. The next three friends kept telling me they had read the first three or four chapters and thought it was wonderful. Great! The first three chapters are wonderful, but what about the rest of the book? I began to wonder if those first chapters were so great, why did my friends never manage to read the rest of the book?

Next, I went to my son. He has professionally edited books, and I think he was a little hurt that I hadn't asked him to read it earlier. But I wanted to wait until I felt it was really the best it could be before I asked his opinion. He did give me some great feedback—on the first fifty pages. And kept telling me he'd read the rest as soon as he had free time.

I'm still waiting.

Finally, I sent the book to another editor I regularly use and paid her. And she got the book back to me within two weeks. She helped me to rethink the last few chapters where I knew I was having problems. I didn't use all her suggestions—*whether using a paid or unpaid editor you always have the option to reject suggested changes.*

While my experience with beta readers was, at best, mixed, I've seen it work for enough other writers that I would suggest you definitely consider using them. Just remember my earlier advice: Too many cooks often only confuse the results. Choose only a couple of trusted beta readers.

Technical Readers

Another excellent reason to use a beta reader is if you have a lot of technical, historical, or other information that you want to ensure are correct. One author I know who writes biographies makes sure to give his manuscript to a couple of additional experts in the field before publishing. They often come up with some new information for him on how things should be worded or where he has made an error that a general proofreader might not catch, such as listing a soldier as a Lieutenant Colonel when he had already been promoted to Colonel at the time mentioned in the book.

No matter how expert you are on a subject, having someone else who is also an expert go over your work is an excellent way to make sure you don't make obvious errors.

Advance Readers

I definitely suggest asking several people to be advance readers for your book. Some of them can be people you know;

others might be experts you don't know but from who would like to receive a review. You might also send your book to review services and newspapers, but we'll cover that in the next chapter.

When choosing advance readers, make sure to do the following:
1. Give them enough time to read the book before the publication date.
2. Be very specific about where, when, and how you would like them to review your book.
3. Find out in what format they would like to receive the book: a paper copy, a PDF, or an e-book.
4. Remind them politely that they have agreed to review the book. Then remind them again if necessary.
5. You cannot ask for a favorable review or give away something in return for the review.

The big lesson I have learned over the years in using both beta readers and advance readers is that everyone promises to read your work, but most of them don't do it. It's just a fact of life; we all tend to put things off.

Action Items

- Make a list of three to five people you would like to ask to be a beta reader.
- If you are ready, ask them to read your book. Remember to give them adequate time to read it.
- Make a list of ten or more people you will ask to be advance readers.

Chapter 16
Using Reviews

> *If nobody talks about books, if they are not discussed or somehow contended with, literature ceases to be a conversation, ceases to be dynamic. Most of all, it ceases to be intimate. It degenerates into a monologue or a mutter. An unreviewed book is a struck bell that gives no resonance. Without reviews, literature would be oddly mute in spite of all those words on all those pages of all those books. Reviewing makes of reading a participant sport, not a spectator sport.*
> *– Patricia Hampfl, writer and memoirist*

I hope your advanced readers have given you a headstart on getting some good reviews on Amazon, and possibly Goodreads and Google Books. Amazon customer reviews are important but also are many other aspects of getting reviews for your book. There are traditional book reviews—those long, thoughtful, critical, *The New York Times*-style reviews. There are also "blurbs," customer reviews on other sites such as Goodreads, and short reviews or testimonials at the front of your book or on the cover. All are excellent ways to bring your book to the attention of a new audience.

The more people who review your book, the greater exposure it has to new and different people who are potential customers. Do not underestimate the power of these types of reviews. Think of them as a form of peer pressure. We are all influenced by what other people are wearing, buying, or talking about.

I know a lot of you just turned your noses up at that idea. "I don't care what other people think. I make my own decisions," you said to yourself. Think again. Do you check *Consumer Reports* before purchasing a big-ticket item? Do you ask your friends for recommendations when you need to find a doctor, dentist, or car mechanic? Have you ever bought a book because you heard other people talking about it? Yes, you are influenced by what other people think. That's why getting your book reviewed is an important technique in selling it.

Pre-Publication Reviews

It's a great idea to have some reviews or testimonials before you publish your book, in addition to friends and family who will post their reviews on Amazon. Who should you ask to give you these additional reviews? The most influential people you know. A review from an unknown person is much less impressive in this case than a review from someone with some credentials. A review from someone whose expertise is totally unrelated to your topic, particularly if it is technical in nature, is also fairly meaningless. Once again, think about your target market. Who is considered a leader in their eyes?

Just Ask

I've spent more hours coaxing writers into asking their heroes for reviews than I can count. "He won't review my book. He's so much more important than I am." That's the line I often hear. It's amazing, though, how many times a simple email asking for a review is answered in the positive.

When you ask, however, make sure you give a deadline date. Even the most well-intentioned person will put things off.

Sometimes the reviewer will ask you to send something specific (three chapters, for instance) or a paper copy. If no special requests are made, send a clean final draft of your book in PDF form. Make sure it is the most complete and error-free copy possible. Have the manuscript checked by a proofreader before you send it to someone to review. A manuscript filled with typos and mistakes won't make a great impression. If this is not the final draft, make that clear to the reviewer.

Where and When to Use Reviews

Of course, you'll want to put a couple of great reviews on the back cover of your book and, if you have gathered enough of them, on the first page as well. You may need to shorten the reviews to just a sentence or two to get them to fit. You can also put lengthier reviews on your website, use them in press releases about your book, and add them to your A+ Content information on Amazon.

Amazon Reviews

We discussed Amazon reviews previously, but they are important enough to mention again. This is when you can call on friends and relatives. Ask everyone you know who reads your book to add a review on Amazon. Good reviews matter. People do read them, and they do influence their decision to buy your book.

Do not only count on random reviews from unknown people who have purchased your book on Amazon.

Send copies of your book and request reviews from potential reviewers on Amazon's Top Reviewers list (http://www.amazon.com/review/top-reviewers). Once again, look for people who review books similar to yours. You are writing a memoir so don't look for a reviewer who only reviews mysteries. Of course, you have no control over what a reviewer says. You may receive a bad review; it's just one of the chances you take as an author.

Give and You Shall Receive

Take the time to review other people's books. Why? Well, first, it is just a thoughtful thing to do. If you like the book, write about it. Second, it is one more way to get your name out there. Post reviews on Amazon. Write reviews on blogs and other public forums where you can add the title of your book and a URL to your website to your signature line.

Send Out Review Copies of Your Book

As soon as you receive copies of your book, send them to reviewers. Figure at least the first fifty books you receive will be given away, not sold. Yes, this hurts. You have just spent a lot of money publishing your book, and you want to start earning it back right away. But remember Marketing Rule Number 4: Every copy of your book that you give away results in approximately ten additional sales. Send out review copies as soon as possible. A new book is news; a six-month-old book is not.

Where to Find Reviewers

Dozens of blogs on the internet focus just on book reviews. Some major newspapers and magazines still have book review columns, and many podcasts are devoted to books. Once again, figure out who your tribe listens to or reads. Are there blogs aimed at your target audience? Send those bloggers copies of your book.

Some authors now distribute complimentary review copies of their books through at least two online sites: goodreads.com and librarything.com. You can request—not demand—reviewers who receive a copy of the book to post a review at Amazon as well as on the website where they received the book. Some reviewers will do this, others will not.

Journal Reviews

Book review journals are often read by librarians and bookstore managers. These people make a lot of their purchasing decisions based on reviews in these journals. Unless you have a major publisher behind you, however, it can be difficult to get your book reviewed in these journals unless you pay for a review. While it is certainly a legitimate marketing technique, it is difficult to accomplish for the average author. If your time is unlimited, it could pay off. But if you are juggling a full-time career and a family, this option should not make your top ten list of marketing strategies to try.

Paid Reviews

There are probably more differing opinions on the value of the paid review than there are journals that place them. *Publishers Weekly* now publishes paid reviews as well as unpaid reviews. Another is *Kirkus Reviews*, one of the biggest reviewers for independent authors. I know several authors who have had excellent results with paid reviews in magazines published by Midwest Book Review.

Paid reviews may have less value than unpaid reviews, but they do still have value. If you are a first-time author, a paid review may be your best chance to get in front of buyers for libraries, bookstores, and other retail outlets. Once again, there is a downside. There is no guarantee a paid reviewer will give your book a good review. It is the only way reviewers and review journals can maintain their credibility, but it also makes this marketing technique a little bit chancy.

Dealing With Negative Reviews

Negative reviews happen. No matter how wonderful your book is, there is someone who will not like it. If they write about it, it can hurt your sales. But there is good news. One or two negative reviews among a group of positive ones will not hurt sales too badly. Reasonable people understand no one can please everyone all the time.

It is difficult—if not impossible—to remove a negative review from the internet. Even if it is removed, you can never remove the negative impression it made in the minds of potential readers. Most blog sites do have policies against abuse and will take down reviews that are malicious or inappropriate. Amazon, for instance, requires reviewers to critique the book rather than express opinions about the author or other unrelated topics. According to its policies, it will delete a review that is "illegal, obscene, threatening, defamatory, invasive of privacy, infringing of intellectual property rights, or otherwise injurious to third parties." If you feel a review of your book falls into one of these categories, you can make a request with the

Community Help department to have the review taken down at community-help@amazon.com.

Ask for Reviews

Who would you like to review your book? Do you have friends, acquaintances, networking contacts, and others who have made a name for themselves in your field? Ask them to review your book before it is published. These blurbs can be used on the back cover of the book, or just before or just after the title page. You should also place them on your website.

Don't be shy. Think of the most well-known people in your field and approach them. If you aren't personally acquainted with them, try to get an introduction through a mutual acquaintance. If you are in the same field, you may want to reference a trade organization or other connection that you share. What's the worst that can happen? The person will say no to you, and you will move on to the next one on your list.

To ask for a review, send an email explaining exactly what you want—a two- or three-sentence review of the book is just fine; in fact, anything over one paragraph can be difficult to place in your book. It is also polite to add a link to a reviewer's website or reference the person's work when you print the review.

For example, identify the author of the review as "Antoinette Brown, author of *The Poor Man's Guide to Great Wines*, www.poormanswine.biz."

Attach a PDF of your book, making sure that it is edited and proofread before you send it. If you are just sending an excerpt, make sure that you explain this; but again, only send edited and proofread material. You want to make a great impression, and you can't do that with unfinished copy or one that has errors.

Give the reviewer a date to return the review. Even the most responsible and well-intentioned people will procrastinate. Don't forget to send a thank-you note when you receive the review, and make sure you send the reviewer a complimentary copy of the book when it is published.

Action Items

- Make a list of the type of reviews you would like for your book.
- Research the people or organizations you want to ask.
- Remember that it takes time for someone to read your book and review it. Plan to ask for reviews at least eight to twelve weeks before your publication date.

Chapter 17
Some Publishing Basics

"After nourishment, shelter, and companionship, stories are the thing we need most in the world."
–Philip Pullman

The time to make decisions on your book is before it is actually printed—not after. I know that sounds obvious, but I've seen many authors regret something about their book after they see it in print. Do the research during the publication process, not after you have a few hundred copies of your book sitting in your garage.

Make sure your publisher or printer offers you the opportunity to see a printed proof copy of your book before several dozen or several hundred copies are printed, ordered, and delivered to you, or are available for sale through an internet bookstore. The time to make those last-minute corrections that will make your book look professional is when you receive your proof so go over your proof copy very carefully.

Even before you receive the proof copy of your book, do some research to make sure the decisions you make on the size and design of your book are the best for you. Once editing is completed you will know how many words your book is and can determine the final size. Every author has a vivid image of their book. It may be small enough to fit in a backpack and be carried everywhere. It may be a workbook with lots of room for the reader to write. It may be thick or thin, include color illustrations, or be a specific shape. Does your vision of your book work with what you have written, the length of the book, your market, and your budget?

The size, design, and overall look of your book are, in fact, very important. Size matters. We buy based on our perception of value, and size is a part of that perception. Every author I have worked with is concerned their book will have enough pages to "feel like a book."

Have you been to a bookstore lately? I mean a physical one, not an online store. This might sound like a silly question, but as more and more bookstores have closed, and as we became used to the convenience of shopping online during the pandemic, many of us stopped going to bookstores. In my town I have to drive almost a half an hour to get to a bookstore, and it is just not in a convenient shopping area for me. So when I went into a Barnes & Noble a few months ago, I realized it was the first time I'd stepping into a bookstore in three years. And I found this bookstore had changed.

There were fewer books on the shelves. The store carried one or two copies of each book, not the half dozen I was used to seeing. There were fewer categories, too. My beloved Westerns were nowhere to be found.

But most important for this chapter, I noticed the size of the books had changed. Most books, even novels, were 6x9", not the smaller 4x6" trade paperback that was standard for novels for so long.

If you haven't been to a bookstore, make sure you visit one. Look at the books in the memoir section and any other category your book might fit into. They are your competition after all. How will your book compete with them?

Look for books with about the same number of pages as your work. Make some notes about the books that you see, including the size, the number of pages, the price, the type of binding, if there are black and white or color photos or graphics. This research can be invaluable in helping you price your book correctly within your market category.

Keep your research and refer to it when you talk with your graphic designer, marketer, printer, and others on your creative team.

Specific information on how to format your book in Microsoft Word, as well as information on printing, pricing, and distribution, can be found in my book *Self-Publishing: You Can Do This! What You Need to Know to Write, Publish & Market Your Book*.

Have a Great Cover

People do judge a book by its cover. We have spoken about finding a professional to develop your cover. Long before you get ready to publish, you need to start thinking about your cover; it is the first impression people will have about your book—when you post on social media, put out a press release and, most importantly, when potential readers click on your book on Amazon or any other book sale website. So why is it so many authors want to skimp on their cover?

When looking for a professional graphic artist, check out what other covers they have created. How do the covers stand up against covers you see in your genre? **You want your cover to look totally unique and, at the same time, fit in with the other covers in its genre.** Book covers for memoirs, mysteries, scholarly books, and romances all have a different look.

Think about promoting your book in more than one genre. Yes, I promote my book *Hibiscus Strong* as a memoir, but it also fits in the categories of "family saga" and "historical fiction" and "women's fiction." My strongest category is "Southern bio." I went through several covers for the book before settling on one. The first cover looked great in the "memoir" category, but it just didn't measure up when compared with covers in the other categories.

Book covers must show well as a postage stamp-sized JPEG. These days many people are shopping for books on their smartphones. That means your cover will show up as one of several on a four-inch by two-inch screen. Don't rely on a template, a friend who will do it free, or any of the other ways you can think of to get a cover as cheaply as possible. A bad cover will hurt your sales. A good cover will draw people to your book and make them want to find out more.

What Is an ISBN?

ISBN stands for International Standard Book Number. If you want to sell a paper book anywhere—including in bookstores, on book websites, in libraries, by book wholesalers, and by distributors—you need one. The ISBN is a unique thirteen-digit number. To make it even more confusing, it corresponds to a ten-digit number. Sometimes when registering your book on a website, you may be asked for your ten-digit number as well as the thirteen-digit number. But all the websites I have encountered automatically convert one to the other. I know this may seem unnecessarily confusing; I only mention it because I have had authors ask me about this ten-digit number. For all practical purposes, your thirteen-digit ISBN does the job.

You will also need a barcode. Stores require the barcode so that they can easily scan their inventory at the cash register. Encoded in the barcode is the price of the book.

The ISBN identifies the publisher of the book. This means you must be careful where you buy it. Amazon and other book websites offer ISBNs at very inexpensive prices. Many first-time authors purchase their ISBN through these sites without understanding the consequences. Let me put it another way. The ISBN is part of the branding of your book. If you "brand" your book with an ISBN that identifies you as an Amazon KDP author, you lose credibility.

Why? Because Amazon will publish anything by anyone who pays and uploads their material. There is no quality control. An Amazon KDP ISBN says, "I don't know what I'm doing."

So where should you purchase your ISBN and barcode? The answer is from www.bowker.com. Bowker offers a variety of "discoverability" resources for authors. I suggest every author go to their website and browse so you can see what is offered and what can be useful to you in marketing your book. An ISBN costs $125 for one book or $295 for ten books. So if you have any idea of publishing more than one book, purchase a group of ten ISBNs. You must, however, purchase your barcode separately, and they cost about $50 each. Bowker often has specials on many of their products so before you need your ISBN, sign up for their newsletter and start watching for specials.

ASIN vs. ISBN

ASIN stands for Amazon Standard Identification Number. When you publish an e-book on Amazon, it will be assigned an ASIN by KDP. You do not have to purchase it. **You do not need an ISBN to publish an e-book on Amazon.** However, you will need one to publish an e-book on other sites.

Your Publishing Name

I strongly recommend you register your ISBNs under a different name than your own, even if you plan to publish only one book. For example, if you already own a business, purchase your ISBNs under the business name. If you do not have a business, create a publishing name. Why? Credibility. Your publishing company appears on all the listings about your book, including the book itself. A book that states "written by Jane Doe and published by Jane Doe" will have less credibility than one that states "written by Jane Doe, published by Deer Park Publishing."

This publishing name is called an "imprint." It does not mean you are establishing a separate business.

Reminder: If you have any questions about the legal or tax implications, check with your attorney or your accountant.

Printers and Distributors

Who is going to print your book? How are you going to get your books to individual customers? You have options. Before we begin to discuss them, here are some important printing terms you should know.

- **Perfect bound:** A widely used soft cover binding method in which the pages and cover are glued together at the spine. Currently the most common soft cover book binding.
- **Saddle stitched:** Saddle stitched books are not actually stitched; they are stapled. Saddle stitch is used for smaller books that do not have enough pages for a spine. This method is often used in children's picture books.

- **Paper weight:** Literally, the weight of a ream of paper; sixty pound paper is most commonly used for interior book pages.
- **Cover stock:** A heavier paper used for the cover of a book. This can come in many weights and is also called card stock.
- **Glossy:** A paper finish for cover stock. It has a glossy coating that shines. Some glossy stock will also have an additional coating, making it shinier and more durable.
- **Matte:** A cover finish that does not have a shine to it, which can be achieved by using a dull, or matte, finish cover stock, or with an additional coating sometimes referred to as "soft touch." Both glossy and matte are perfectly acceptable for books. It's all about the look you want to achieve.

Action Items

When thinking about how you want your book to look, start with a little at-home market research. Go to your bookshelf and pick out three books that you particularly like; they can be on any topic. Ask yourself these questions about each one.
- What are the height and width?
- How many pages does it have?
- What do I find appealing about the cover?
- Why do I like this book?
- Are there things I don't like about it?

Next, go to a local brick-and-mortar bookstore, and do the same research.

Chapter 18
Amazon KDP vs. Ingram Spark

> *Today, we have our own concentrations of economic power. Instead of Standard Oil, U.S. Steel, the Union Pacific Railroad, and J. P. Morgan and Company, we have Amazon, Google, Apple, Facebook, and Microsoft.*
> —George Packer

The easiest way to get a large number of copies of your book is to use Amazon Kindle Direct Publishing as your printer. Note: I said "printer," not "publisher." **You are your own publisher. You own your ISBN and your copyright.** But KDP does an excellent job of printing books and shipping them to you in larger quantities at discount prices.

There are some caveats here. KDP does not sell to individual bookstores at discount prices. If your mind is set on working with bookstores, you need to have your books in stock and personally sell them and deliver them. This approach will make your final profit extremely small. Bookstores want to make money, too.

Ingram: Lightning Source and Spark

Another printing and distribution service is Ingram Content Group, the largest book wholesaler in the world. Lightning Source and Ingram Spark are their divisions that work with small publishers and individual authors. Most independent authors will work with Spark.

Working with Lightning Source or Spark will make your book available through other book retail sites including Barnes & Noble (B&N), Books-A-Million (BAM), and Google Books. It will not necessarily make the books available in B&N and

BAM retail stores, but they will be available online.

Before making your decision, explore all the websites, read everything, and decide which service is best for you.

Ingram vs. Amazon

About ten years ago I always advised authors to upload their paper books to Ingram and bypass Amazon KDP. After all, if a book was uploaded through Lightning Source or Ingram Spark, it showed up automatically on Amazon, and the printing and other distribution choices were better.

About five years later I found that Amazon had improved. Because it was significantly less expensive than Spark, I began recommending that authors upload paper books exclusively to Amazon unless they were going to seriously go after the bookstore market.

These days I recommend that authors upload their books to both Ingram Spark and Amazon. Why the redundancy?

1. Putting your book on Ingram Spark gives you access to a wider variety of online book sellers and makes it much more likely that your book will be listed in Google Books. This added visibility greatly increases your Search Engine Optimization (SEO), as well as gives readers greater choice in where they purchase your book.

2. Amazon doesn't play nice with other book distributors. I have noticed that books uploaded only to Ingram and not also to Amazon often show fewer books available and longer delivery times. Showing that only a few books are in stock does not generally encourage people to buy, and showing a book as out of stock is a definite turnoff to buyers. It is easy enough to upload your book to both Ingram Spark and Amazon KDP.

Cost of Uploading and Other Considerations

There is one more factor to think about when deciding which distributor you will use when you upload your book. Amazon KDP is free. There is no charge when you upload a book. There is no charge when or if you make changes to your manuscript. There are charges if you decide to use certain additional services, such as hiring an editor. But with that exception—and you are not required to use any of the additional services—Amazon is free.

Ingram Spark is also free to upload, and it is free to make changes *for the first thirty days after you upload*. After that the company charges if you make changes to your manuscript or cover, including change fees if the cover or manuscript is rejected for technical reasons. If using Ingram Spark, make sure you get all the details right the first time because these changes can add up.

Both KDP and Spark charge for printed proof copies. Amazon's costs tend to be slightly less for this service.

There are a couple of additional details to know before you upload your books to KDP and Spark. **Always upload your book to Spark first.** Remember I mentioned that Amazon doesn't play well with others? In this case it is Spark that doesn't play nicely. If you upload your book to KDP first, Spark will list your ISBN as "already taken" so you will not be able to upload your book. You will have to contact their help desk, get a lot of runaround, and then, with any luck, get an exception made for your book. It can be very frustrating, and it leads me to the next item to think about.

If you need assistance or have questions about anything with your uploading, genres, covers, and other details, Amazon's help desk is great. To access it, click on "Help" at the top of the page and you will be directed to the Help page. It offers a lot of useful information. If you don't see an answer to your question, scroll to the bottom of the page and click on "Contact us,." which takes you to another page that asks you to select the area in which you need help. Then you have the option to receive a response by email or by phone. I usually use the phone option unless I need to upload an example for the help desk to look at. Responses are usually within an hour or two by email and within fifteen minutes by phone.

And then there is Spark. If you need help you must email. You will get a "ticket," and within a day you will get a response. I have to say that I usually find their responses more confusing.

The bottom line on KDP versus Spark: Each has its uses. Before you upload your book to either service, think about your goals. If you never plan to market your book to bookstores, and you don't care that your book is only available on one platform, KDP will probably be fine. But if you think that in the future you may change your mind and want to work with bookstores, or you find that a lot of your readers would prefer to use another site to purchase your book, upload to Spark first. It is much easier to make this decision ahead of time than to try to change it later.

Other Printers and Distributors

Dozens of printers nationwide specialize in books, and hundreds of other local printers can help you with part or all your project, including your interior layout and cover design. You may decide to use a book printer to print additional copies of your book for you to sell at seminars, book festivals, and other events. Check their prices carefully. They range from excellent to terrible.

Local print shops may tell you they can print perfect bound books but are really sending your project out to someone, which will increase your cost. If you are lucky enough to find a local printer who can print your books in-house, you can save a lot on shipping costs, making this a viable option. If your book is saddle stitched, your local options will greatly increase.

Make sure the books you get from different printers look very similar, if not identical. Paper weight and cover stock choices should be the same whether your reader orders your book online, buys it in a bookstore, or buys it from you through your website or at an in-person event.

There are also printers who specialize in distribution. They will print a few hundred books and keep them on hand at their warehouse, then send them out individually, saving you a lot of time. This approach can work well if you plan to set up a large pre-order campaign.

You have a lot of details to think about when it comes to picking a printer and distributor. Do your research. Ask a lot of questions. Make sure you are clear about how you want your book to look—including its style, its size, and its price—long before you see that first proof copy. That way you won't be disappointed when the big day finally arrives.

Action Item

Set up an account at both Amazon KDP and Ingram Spark several weeks before you need to upload your book. Take the time to read through the FAQ sections and tutorials that each site offers. Making yourself familiar with the site will make it easier to upload your book when you are ready.

Chapter 19
E-Books & Audiobooks

What is an e-book? That may seem like a pretty simplistic question but ask ten people what an e-book is, and you'll probably get ten different answers. The best answer is deceptively simple: An e-book is any book that can be transferred to, and read on, an electronic device. It can be a PDF or an .epub file, to name the most common formats currently in use for e-books.

Formatting Your E-book

Formatting your e-book means first knowing a thing or two about e-books. E-books do not have traditional set pages. Pages change depending on the size of the e-reader and the font size the reader chooses. As a person with poor eyesight, one of my favorite things about using an e-reader is I can increase the font to the size most comfortable for me.

E-readers also have a limited number of fonts, but some allow the reader to choose the font they prefer. The reader can also choose to increase or decrease the spacing between lines. This feature means readers have more choice in how a book will look than they do with traditional paper books, while the author or publisher has less. Most e-reader software has a nightlight setting, or the print can be changed from black-on-white to white-on-black for ease in reading under different lighting conditions.

It is essential to the creation of a professional-looking e-book to have an understanding of the e-book reading experience. **The first step you should take before publishing your book as an e-book is to download the free software onto your computer, tablet, or mobile device and read a few e-books.**

Next, decide if you will format the book yourself or hire a service. I know many writers prefer to do the formatting themselves, but if this is not something you want to do, you can hire an e-book formatting service to help you. Take the time to do it right; read and check your work before you submit it. Just as with a paper book, nothing reduces your credibility and professionalism more quickly than a poorly formatted e-book.

If you have an older book that is only available to you as a paper document, you can quickly convert it to a text document using Optical Character Reader (OCR) software. Adobe Acrobat Professional is one program that has this option. Be careful if you are using OCR software, however, because while it is a great timesaver, it is also prone to specific errors, such as confusing the letters "m," "n," and "r." I've read e-books in which certain letters always appear as capitals or in italics, or certain words are consistently misspelled. These are small but annoying errors to the reader and take some of the joy out of reading. Use the OCR software. It is excellent; just make sure you proof your work.

Amazon KDP makes it easy for the do-it-yourselfer. Once your paper book is formatted and proofed, with a few additional steps your Word document will be ready to upload to Amazon, and software on the site will convert it to an e-book. Here are the steps.

1. If you do not have a Contents page in your paper book, add one now, putting in only the chapter numbers and titles. Do not worry about page numbers. Remember: They don't count in an e-book. If you do have a Contents page already in the book, remove the page numbers. Add all additional content on your Contents page such as Acknowledgments, any maps or important tables, and the About the Author page.

2. Make sure you are in "compatibility mode," which saves the document as a Word 1997-2003 document.

3. Start with the Contents page. Highlight the words "Contents," click on the insert tab, then click on "bookmark." In the dialogue box type "ref_TOC" and click "add." Go to each chapter page, highlight the chapter title, click on bookmark, and type in the chapter. **You cannot use any spaces.** I suggest you use an abbreviation such as

CH1, CH2, and so on. Go through the entire book, and do this for all chapters and any other content you want the reader to easily locate.

4. Now you are ready to create your links. Go back to the Contents page and hyperlink it to each individual chapter page. To do this, highlight the chapter title on the Contents page. On the "Insert" tab, open the dialogue box marked "Link." On the left, click on the "place in this document" box. This brings up the bookmarks you just created. Select the bookmark that corresponds to the highlighted chapter, then click "OK." The link should turn blue and be underlined if you have done it correctly.

5. Next, link the chapters back to the Contents page so that readers can click back and forth if they wish. Go back to each chapter page and hyperlink back to "ref_TOC."

6. Always check a few of your links to make sure they are working.

7. Go through your document and make sure any references you have to websites or email addresses are also linked. This is easy. Just type the URL (the address for a website), hit one space, and the link should be active.

Now you are ready to upload your book.

Pricing Your E-book

Pricing for e-books has changed dramatically in the past few years. Several years ago when e-books first came out, most were capped at a flat rate of $9.99, which could either be much too high a price or much too low, depending on the particular book. But as competition for e-book sales increased among the bookstore websites, that changed. Prices now vary from book to book, and authors and publishers have control. Make sure—no matter who your publisher is—you have control of your e-book pricing and promotions.

I notice that some publishers, particularly university publishing houses, price their e-books at only a few dollars less than the paper book price. They also don't do e-book promotions. If you have the opportunity to publish your paper book with a traditional publisher, I strongly suggest you attempt to keep the e-book rights, as well as the pricing and uploads, under your own control. Being realistic, you probably won't be able to write this stipulation into your contract, but it never hurts to ask. Currently, $3.99 or $4.99 are the most common prices for e-books. That gives you room to run great price promotions later.

Should All Books Be E-books?

As e-readers become more popular and are able to do more, the list of books that should not be formatted as an e-book is growing shorter. Readers are more likely to purchase fiction than nonfiction as an e-book, but some nonfiction does quite well electronically. Technology and computer books are obvious choices for e-books. Business books also do well.

Interestingly, while women were the first to adopt e-readers, today the largest demographic is men ages thirty-five to fifty-four years. Now that color has come to e-readers, children's picture books are becoming more popular. Since the pandemic, children have become even more familiar and comfortable with reading online.

The question today is not who should publish an e-book, but who should not.

1. If you are writing a workbook or journal, an e-book will only work if you do some rewriting and reformatting, taking out the original journaling pages or question-and-answer sections and changing the book to state something such as "on a separate sheet of paper write..." In fact, one author I know published her workbook as an e-book on Amazon and was told to take it down. The wording in the email was quite strong. It stated that the content or formatting of the workbook was not appropriate for an e-book and if the author did not take it down, all her books would be removed from Amazon. Since she was selling more than 100 books a month, the answer was obvious. Make life easy on yourself. If your content will not work well as

an e-book, don't try to make it one.

2. If your book contains a large number of graphics, charts, or photographs, consider the fact that while new e-readers may enhance these elements, they will not reproduce well on older e-readers. Your readers are using a wide variety of devices, some old and some new. Your book must be compatible with all of them. It can also be prohibitively expensive to format this type of book as an e-book.

Some Final Notes

The biggest advantage of an e-book is people can find your book, choose it, purchase it, and begin reading instantly. Both e-books and paper books should have a place in your marketing strategy. As you make your decision on creating a paper book, an e-book, or both, look again at your target reader and your marketing plan. The age of the reader, the type of book you are writing, and the type of marketing you plan to do should all be part of your decision.

E-books are covered under the exact same intellectual property laws as paper books. Make sure you always copyright your work, no matter what format you publish it in.

You want to be paid for the e-books you sell on the various websites where they are listed. Each site has slightly different registration rules. You will need to enter your banking information for Electronic Funds Transfer (EFT). Read the directions and rules carefully on each site, and follow them scrupulously, then keep track of your sales and your bank transfers.

Audiobooks

Audiobook sales have increased sharply ever since the Pandemic. In 2020 they generated more than $1.2 billion in revenue. In the same year e-books made only $983 million in total revenue.[1] Using just this statistic it looks like audiobooks

---

[1] https://goodereader.com/blog/audiobooks/audiobook-trends-and-statistics-for-2020

are selling a lot more and making a lot more money for authors than e-books, doesn't it? In fact, it looks like you need to go out and turn your book into an audiobook right now.

Well, maybe you do. And maybe you don't. Here is something else to think about. In 2020 printed book sales amounted to **750.89 million units** while "more than **71,000 audiobooks**" were sold in the United States. So even though audiobooks were the fastest growing part of the book market, they are still lagging far behind paper book and e-books. And the additional expense of creating an audiobook means most authors will not recoup the money they spend on making one.

Are Audiobooks for You?

Once again, we must look at your audience and your purpose. Why have you decided you need an audiobook?

"My best friend only reads audiobooks and tells me everyone is reading them" is not a good enough reason to create an audiobook. If you look at the statistics on the previous page, you'll have to acknowledge that your friend is an outlier, and you may be making an audiobook that only one or two people will read.

However, if a large segment of your audience tells you they are interested in an audiobook, you may want to consider it. I worked recently on a book with an audience that was the visually impaired. If this is your target market, you definitely should create an audiobook.

Who Reads Audiobooks?

The average audiobook users are men, between eighteen and thirty-four years of age. They are affluent. They listen to at least four audiobooks a year. They say they listen for both entertainment and information so both fiction and nonfiction books will work for this demographic. They listen while commuting, working, or exercising. But while they listen to only four audiobooks per year, they may also be reading books in other formats.

Using Amazon ACX

Amazon ACX is Amazon's audiobook version of KDP. After speaking with several people, it seems to be the most cost-effective way to create an audiobook. It may or may not be the best way. Users can receive royalties of up to forty percent. The website is designed as a "marketplace" where authors put out their requirements for a book narrator and voice artists bid for the job. You can make an arrangement to pay upfront for production or you can contract a royalty-sharing arrangement. Books can be made available on Audible.com and iTunes as well as Amazon. This is a different arrangement than Amazon has made for any of its other formats. Your book may also be eligible for the Whispersync functionality for Amazon e-books, which allows readers to switch from reading to listening.

- When working with ACX you can choose your own narrator or "producer" who narrates the book and makes sure that it is a retail-ready audiobook.
- It is possible to narrate your own book.
- Currently, you must live in the United States, the United Kingdom, Canada, or Ireland to use ACX.
- You can choose royalties of forty percent, twenty percent, or twenty-five percent, depending on which distribution options you choose as well as what type of payment you set up with your producer.
- You will receive monthly royalties from Amazon, in the same way in which you receive royalties from other formats.

Pricing Audiobooks

The retail price for audiobooks is generally slightly higher than for paper books. Your audience does recognize the additional work that goes into producing this type of product. But you have little control of how your book is priced. Each retailer, Kobo, Apple, Amazon, etc., sets their own price for you book at it may be different on each site.

Amazon generally prices audio books based on length, with books under an hour priced at under $7; 1 to 3 hours: $7-$10; 3 to 5 hours: $10 - $20, 5-0 hours: $15 - $25, and over 20 hours, $25-35. These are general guidelines, and prices may vary.

Making Changes

The beauty of e-books is that they can easily be changed. Find a typo? Upload a corrected version. Want to add another chapter? Upload a new version. (No, I really don't recommend this but it can be done financially, and sometimes it should be done.) But with audiobooks, it's one and done. You just can't afford to redo an entire recording because you want to make a change in Chapter 13. And once you have that audiobook, you shouldn't make changes to your e-book either because they are often linked.

Now that you have learned a few of the basics about audiobooks, should your book be produced as one? The decision is up to you.

Action Items

- Get the Kindle app, download a free e-book, and read it. Notice the differences between formatting for a paper book and formatting for an e-book.
- Download an audiobook, and spend some time listening to it. Notice what you like and dislike about it.

Chapter 20
Marketing Basics

Stopping advertising to save money is like stopping your watch to save time.
—Henry Ford

You've done it! Finally, after months or even years spent writing and editing your memoir—not to mention living it first, you have chosen a cover design, debated over type fonts, suffered through proofreading and corrections, and dealt with all the usual setbacks and delays of a complex project—you have your memoir in hand. It is beautiful. It is your baby. You want everyone in the world to read it, and you're sure that as soon as a couple of book reviewers find it, you'll head straight to the top of the best seller charts.

Unless you market your book wisely, though, only your mother and a few of your family, friends, and colleagues will buy a copy. **Do you know how many copies the average book sells? Between 200 and 500.** That statistic includes every author from internationally famous ones such as Stephen King and J.K. Rowling to the John Doe who sells fifteen copies of his book on the history of postage stamps to his philatelist club.

So how do you help your book rise above the pack and get noticed when millions of individual book titles are published in the United States each year? I recently heard a marketing guru say that it takes two years of consistent marketing for a book to gain traction and become a solid seller. Notice he didn't say "bestseller," but "solid seller." In other words, a book that reliable sells month after month.

Your Purpose—Again

The first step in deciding how to market your book is to look one more time at your purpose in writing it. Yes, I know I sound like a broken record on this subject, and right now you are thinking "of course, my purpose is to sell as many books as possible." But is it really? Unless you are clear on why you are doing something, how will you know if you have achieved the results you are looking for? Your purpose in writing your book will be a driving force in how you market it.

Ten Marketing Rules

What are the most important things to remember when marketing? The list is as varied as the number of marketing experts you ask. These are my Top Ten Marketing Rules for selling books. I try to keep them in mind while marketing both my own books and those of other authors.

1. **Marketing a book is marketing you.**

You are selling your expertise, your knowledge, and your ability to tell a story and to engage your audience. You aren't just selling your book; you are selling yourself. This is particularly true of memoir.

2. **The day you stop marketing your book is the day it stops selling.**

If you aren't telling people about your book, they won't go looking for it on their own. There is no "write it and they will come." You have to give your potential readers a roadmap to find it.

3. **Selling to everyone is selling to no one.**

Your target market is your "sweet spot," the eighty percent of the market most likely to purchase your book. Yes, your book may appeal to a wide variety of people, but which group is the most likely to buy your book? What traits do they share? Where will you find them? How can you let them know that your book is available for sale?

4. **Don't be a miser; give your books away.**

I recently read an interesting statistic. One book given away can encourage ten book sales. This is a very important point to remember. Authors become very cost-conscious with their books; they are afraid to give away that sample copy. Sow your books like seeds on the wind—you never know what fruit they will bring.

5. Depend on yourself; no one cares about your book like you do.

YOU are the person who cares the most about your product. YOU are the person who ultimately must make the decisions about which marketing techniques to use. If it doesn't feel right, don't do it.

6. Hire experts to help you.

This seems to be the opposite advice of Marketing Rule Number 5, but it is not. Yes, you are the person who cares the most about your product, and you should make the final decisions. But you also cannot do it all or be an expert in everything. Hire the experts you need in public relations, marketing, and social media. Spending your money wisely will bring you returns in sales and recognition for you and your book.

7. There is no overnight success.

The media love to tout the overnight success story, but if you really look hard, you'll find years of study and hard work went into most overnight successes.

8. Don't give up.

Pick a marketing technique and try it for several months. If it doesn't work, try another technique, and then another. Don't just try one marketing technique and, if it doesn't bring you the results you want in a week or two, give up. I've known too many authors who do this, then say to themselves, "Well, that didn't work. I guess no one wants to buy my book." Instead of giving up on your book, find a new way to market it.

9. Don't try to do it all at once.

Here is a corollary to Marketing Rule Number 8: There are hundreds of different marketing techniques you can use—don't try to do them all at once unless you have a large publicity staff behind you. Do some research, pick three or four techniques you think will work best for you and your book, and do them well.

10. Always look professional.

This goes for both you and your book. You wouldn't go to a

business event wearing torn jeans and a t-shirt. Why would you try to save money by skipping steps on your book's appearance? Pay for a professional editor, proofreader, and graphic artist. Make sure your book looks as professional as you do.

Your Marketing Plan

Before you can effectively market your book, you need a plan. Without one, your marketing will feel helter-skelter, and probably bring you very few positive results. Start by thinking creatively about how to market your book using both digital and in-person marketing. Everything from tweeting and blogging to good old-fashioned networking should be considered. One author I know recently sold 200 books in the first ten days after publication using only word-of-mouth marketing and networking in her community. Another author is great at selling her book to individuals with whom she starts conversations in restaurants, parking lots, or on the hiking trail. With a good plan, you can do this and more, too.

Here is a sample marketing plan to get you started. Put a checkmark next to the ideas you think will work for you. Use a separate sheet of paper to add additional ideas of your own.

__Send news releases to local, regional, and national publications about your book.

__Send copies of your book review websites.

__Have a party. Invite your friends, family, and business associates. Announce the event to local media.

__Have a Zoom book launch. Market it on Facebook. Offer your book for sale in your Facebook invitation.

__Place a book trailer (a one-minute or less video for your book) on YouTube and other internet sites to advertise your book.

__Blog and tweet about your area of expertise.

__Develop add-on products that sell your book. If you're a fiction writer, for instance, can your book be adapted for a computer game?

__These days most books are not sold in traditional bookstores. Make a list of gift shops and boutiques selling items related to your book.

Now, using these ideas, create your own marketing plan.

Create a Budget

Once you've decided on how to market your book, ask yourself which portions of your plan you can do yourself and which ones will need the help of a book publicist, marketer, or social media expert. Sure, you can probably write a news release that will get you into the local newspaper, but if your goal is to get an interview on a national news show, you will need help getting there. No one starts out with an interview in *The Wall Street Journal* or on a national talk show. Get your feet wet with local marketing, then regional marketing, then go for the national audience.

Set up a timeline and a budget; be realistic about it. Marketing costs money, but it can pay for itself in increased sales of your book and increased recognition of you as an expert in your field. Here are two samples of an easy checklist you can use to develop your own marketing plan and budget.

Marketing activity: Press release for local publications, TV, and radio announcing the publication of a book by a local author

Steps:

1. Find or create a list of all appropriate media outlets in the county.

2. Identify the proper person at each outlet and the person's preferred contact method.

3. Write a news release.

4. Distribute the news release via email and snail mail. Include copies of your book or book excerpts when appropriate.

5. Follow up with telephone calls.

Budget: $200 for postage; copies of book to be distributed to the media

Marketing activity: Hold a seminar on your book topic
Steps:
1. Develop an outline for a one- to two-hour seminar.
2. Find a meeting place to hold it (for example, local libraries and restaurants are good locations).
3. Set a price for the event based on the cost of the meeting place, marketing materials, seminar materials, and refreshments.
4. Decide whether to sell your book after the seminar or include it in the workshop price.
5. Announce your seminar through your website, newsletter, and news releases.
Budget: A seminar budget can be anywhere from the cost of materials to $1,000 or more for an elaborate setup. Use the checklist on the following pages to develop your own marketing plan and budget.

Use the above checklist to develop your own marketing plan. First, choose a specific activity, write down the steps needed to complete it, and then determine your budget. The final step is to make sure your budget is realistic. If you need to hire additional help to host that seminar or write the press release, find out how much it will cost before you start announcing plans.

Action Item

Use the ideas in this chapter to create a year-long marketing plan for your book.

Chapter 21
Launch Your Book

Your life story is a gift, and it should be treated as such.
–Emily Gordon

It's finally here. The day you have dreamed about for months, maybe even for years. A carton—or two, or three, or six—arrives on your doorstep, and your book is here.

Now, what are you going to do with it? You want to go right out and start selling it. Instead, plan to have your books arrive at least a month before the official launch date. That will give you time to take care of all the final details for your launch events, as well as send out advance copies to reviewers and make sure all the details have been taken care of. I've been through plenty of book launches in which I watched the author sweat it out waiting for the books to arrive the day before the book launch. Believe me, it's no fun.

Let's start by going back over the basics. I hope you've already handled most of these items several weeks, if not months, before your book arrives. But if not, now is the time to take care of them.

Where Can People Buy Your Book?

Is your book listed on a variety of bookselling websites such as barnesandnoble.com, amazon.com, and booksamillion.com? If not, now is the time to make sure these listings have been uploaded and are correct. Maximize your Amazon listing with an Author Page and A+ Content copy. You can, and should, have your book listed on Amazon before the date the book will be shipped; it's another way people can pre-order it.

You need to write a basic press release about your book. Once you have your first press release, it can then be edited slightly for different media and different events. A basic press release should be no longer than one page. Make sure you add anything that a reporter might find particularly interesting, a "hook" to hang a feature story on. Is the book set in the local area? Does it discuss a local historic event? Are there other unique touches you can think of? What makes you a unique and interesting interview?

Also include your contact information and paragraphs about you, your book, and coming events such as a book signing or workshop.

Send Out Review Copies

I know that you want to start making money on your book right away, but some of the first copies of your book are going to be given away, not sold. Look over the media list you created and decide to whom you should send a full media kit, to whom you will send a copy of the book for review, and who just needs a simple press release.

You may decide to send the editor of your local newspaper a review copy as well as a complete press kit. Regional and national media will probably need only the press kit. Book reviewers should definitely receive a copy of the book—they can't review it if they haven't read it.

Send out advanced reader copies to your friends, family, and fans. Ask them specifically to review the book on Amazon, Google Books, Goodreads, and other websites. For more information on planning this type of book launch, check out the chapter on the 100 Review Book Launch plan in my book *How to Sell Your Book Today: Focus your book marketing for the new digital economy.*

Press Release vs. Press Kit

I have mentioned "press release" and "press kit," and I hope I haven't confused you too much. There is a difference. A press release is just one part of an overall press kit. Sometimes you just need to send the release; at other times you will want to send the entire kit.

If your book has been out for awhile and most of the media you are targeting has already seen the entire kit, you may want to send just a press release to announce a new event or a new goal reached.

If your book is brand new and no one knows about it, an entire kit will be more helpful and is a better way in which to sell your story to the media.

If you look up "press kit for authors" online, you may find several different opinions and lists of what should be included. Here is mine.

1. Press release
2. Short author bio
3. Back cover synopsis
4. JPEG files of the book and of yourself
5. Reviews if you have them
6. Links to articles or videos about you and/or your book
7. The title, price, ISBN, and formats in which the book is available

I've put a sample press release in the resources section at the back of this book.

Host an Event—or Three

Book signings, book launch parties, seminars, and workshops—in person or online—are essential events. Use them all to promote your book in the first few months after it is published. You have just accomplished something fantastic so celebrate. Some events, such as a launch party where you are footing the bill, can be by invitation only—everyone's budget is limited after all.

Being an invitation only event doesn't mean that you should only invite family and close friends. Invite business colleagues, referral partners, and, of course, anyone who helped you with your book such as the editor or graphic artist. Plan to sell your book during the event. Have a table set up to display the book and accept sales; designate someone to take the money and hand out the book while you as the author act as host, network, give a short speech or reading from your book, and sign copies. Even if the event is private, invite the press, and also send a follow-up press release and photos of the event to local media.

If you are hosting a public event, such as a book signing at a local store, a seminar, or a workshop, make sure you send out as many flyers, press releases, email invitations, or other types of advertising as you can to attract a large crowd.

Event Follow-Up

The great thing about an event is you never know who you will meet or reconnect with—even if, or possibly especially if, it is your own event and you have set the guest list. After all, everyone who attends your book signing or launch party presumably has come to meet you. You may not have a chance to spend as much time as you like with every guest so have a guest book at the launch to make sure you get names and contact information for everyone who attends.

Follow up with written notes thanking everyone who helped make your event a success. Send a note or email to anyone you would like to get to know better and, if appropriate, set up an appointment.

Don't forget to post some photos of the event on your Facebook page, your website, and other social media, and tag the photos with the names of the people in them. People love to look at pictures of themselves and their friends. It is one more way to bring people to your website and keep you and your book in front of your audience.

Podcasts and Television Interviews

Podcast hosts love to interview authors. There are literally thousands of podcasts online, and many run several different shows a week. That's a lot of airtime to fill. Just as with book reviews, you can find podcasts to fit almost any niche market you can think of, and it is often the best way for beginners on the speaking circuit to gain name recognition outside their local area.

Some podcasts are audio only; some include video. Make sure you know whether you'll be seen on-air or not. You don't want to show up in you pajamas and find out you are live on the internet.

Television can be more difficult to break into. There are fewer television stations with less time devoted to talk shows than radio. However, just because it is difficult doesn't mean you shouldn't try. Do more research before you get started. Find out who on the staff actually chooses the guests and direct your query to that person.

Sometimes you get lucky, and the book you have just written is on a topic that hits the news. For example, a book on airline safety that hits the press a few weeks before a major air disaster or a biography of a celebrity who gets arrested, divorced, or dies. It sounds macabre, but let's face it: Most breaking news is often about the less-than-pleasant events in life. If a book you have written relates to a current news event, use it. Call your local television station and let them know you have information to share.

When you sign up for the site, emails describing the stories reporters are working on arrive a few times a day. The secret is to learn to quickly scan the entries for reporters who are working on stories in your niche. Then reply to the email with a short summary of how you can help the reporter. Do not give up if you do not find anything in the first few weeks, and make sure you follow the rules of etiquette for the sites.

YouTube interviews are becoming more and more common. Again, the beauty of these types of interviews is that they live pretty much forever on the internet. Make sure that you ask if you can have a copy of the file so that you can put it on your own YouTube channel. That way you know that the interview will continue to be easily available for you to share.

No matter if your video interview is being recorded in a television studio or from your home through Zoom or another recording app, make sure that you are dressed appropriately. Your appearance, background, and quality of your sound should all be excellent.

How to Look Great in a Zoom Interview

Do wear bright colors and put on makeup, but avoid stripes, plaids, and large prints, which can be distracting on a small screen. Do wear pants—real pants, not pajama bottoms. For the most part they won't be seen, but you still occasionally stand up and move around when on a Zoom call. You don't want to be caught in torn PJ bottoms.

Do wear jewelry, and I don't just mean the ubiquitous iPhone earbuds. But also definitely consider wearing them. They will block out background sounds. Yes, since the pandemic sent everyone home to work, we've gotten used to seeing animals, kids, spouses, and others on interviews. And while occasionally it is cute and charming, it always distracts the interviewer, and the viewers, from the message you are trying to present. So get out the earbuds and learn to use them.

Do smile and make eye contact with the screen. You may be interacting with several people on a panel discussion, only a host, or be full screen talking to an unseen audience. No matter which it is, look at your camera. It will help people feel that you are interested in them.

Don't fidget and wiggle around. Try not to look at yourself and fuss with your hair. Do find a comfortable chair to sit in.

Your background is very important. You are not practicing for the Witness Protection Program so make sure that your lighting is optimum and does not overshadow or darken your face. A strong light behind you puts your face in a shadow. For the best effect make sure you are lighted from the side front. The worst lighting combines a window behind the person with a light behind the shoulder. The person watching you from the other side of the camera will only see the glare of light and can often feel as if they are in an interrogation room.

Think about your background. Bookshelves are always nice if they are reasonably neat and organized. A desk is good. The special photographic backgrounds that can be used on Zoom are problematic. I've seen some great ones, but if you are only using a free connection, you may find yourself fading in and out rather as if you have a bad transporter connection on Star Trek.

Before your interview check your equipment and your internet connections, even if you have done many interviews in this way. Just a little preplanning will go a long way to giving your interview presence a more professional appearance.

Action Plan

- Make a list of all the activities you want to do for your book launch.
- Begin planning at least three months before your book launch. It will take that long to set up press interviews, podcasts, or an in-person event.

Chapter 22
Keep the Sales Going

A book is a gift you can open again and again.
–Garrison Keillor

There was a time, not too long ago, when books were seen as something ephemeral. Traditional book publishers put out a book, heavily promoted it for three to six months, and then moved on to the next book, leaving the first one to languish on bookstore sales tables and remainder bins.

Authors, of course, have never liked this method of marketing, and as authors and small, independent publishing houses have become more prominent, they have come up with a different technique. It's called "wag the long tail." This phrase means you want to find ways to keep selling your book for several years—not just several months.

So how do you do this? You keep right on marketing. Remember Marketing Rule Number 2? The day you quit marketing your book is the day it quits selling. Well, the corollary is also true: As long as you continue to market your book, it will continue to sell.

Salespeople know it as "ABC"—always be closing. Remind people that you and your book are still out there. Keep up the social networking, continue to write your blog, and book more seminars and public speaking engagements.

When your book first comes out, no one has yet read it so it may be easier to rack up sales in the first few months. Once the majority of your tribe has bought your book, you can't expect sales to maintain the same pace. Unlike commodities such as food and clothing, once we have purchased one copy of a book (maybe two if we give one as a gift), we never need to purchase that book again.

This does not, however, mean you should stop promoting your book just because you have maxed out sales to your family, friends, and fans. There are always new people moving into your sphere of influence—people you have not met before or people who have just become interested in the subject you are writing about. You may not sell hundreds books a month, but ten or fifteen sales a month will add to your bottom line. The trick is to maintain visibility even when you don't have a new book on the market. After all, it takes time to produce a book. You can't put a new one out each month.

Brick-and-mortar bookstores don't have the space for the slow-but-steady seller. To make money they need to specialize in hot, new titles. Online stores, however, have unlimited shelf space. Make sure your book is available on Amazon and other book selling websites, but think about other types of stores, too.

Is there an online specialty store catering to your target market? If your book is about a particular sport, particularly a smaller sport such as lacrosse or rowing, there are online retailers devoted specifically to them. Crafters and hobbyists of all kinds have their own websites. Fiction writers can benefit from this technique, too. There are websites devoted to romance, mystery, and science fiction, as well as other genres. Do the research, approach the site's owners, and see if you can sell your book, post a blog article, or purchase an advertisement.

Watch the News

Is there a breaking news event that ties in with your subject matter? Don't hesitate. Put out a press release immediately, and call attention to the fact that: (1) you are an expert in the field, and (2) you have written a book on the subject.

Calendar tie-ins can also generate news. What annual events can be used to promote your book? If your book is aimed at women, it would make a great Mother's Day gift. A book about planning a wedding should have a special promotion every June. Ghost stories sell in October, and anything about Irish heritage does well around St. Patrick's Day.

What calendar events can you use to promote your

book? Don't just think of the big days, such as Christmas or Valentine's Day. There are hundreds of special days, from the well-known such as Arbor Day to National Grammar Day (bet you didn't know about that one), that you can capitalize on. Don't forget special weeks and months such as Women's History Month and African American History Month, too. Find yours and promote your book.

Seminars and Events

Do you give speeches or hold seminars and workshops—online or in person? Make sure you always have your book available to sell at any event where you are speaking. The audience is obviously interested in what you have to say so make sure they have the opportunity to take your book home with them.

Use your book as a giveaway to add value to a seminar, workshop, or other promotion. "If you sign up for my seminar now, you'll receive my book as part of the package." It's a tried-and-true marketing technique—and it works.

This also works for e-books. You can offer the e-book as part of that "sign up for my event" promotion. Or once you have two books available, do a free promotion on your first book, particularly if it is part of a series. You are only giving your book away for one week, and readers will get hooked on book one and immediately purchase book two. I speak from experience here—not as an author but as a reader. I will often use a free e-book promotion to try out a new author. There are many times I'm so hooked that immediately on finishing the first book, I go to Amazon and purchase the second.

Two-for-One and Other Offers

What other products do you sell? Promote your book in conjunction with one of your other products. For example, Book A sells alone for $15. Book B sells alone for $10. If purchased separately, your customer will have spent $25. Sell the books together for $20. Everyone wants a bargain. You'll be amazed at how many people will buy the two together. Think of the packages you see at most bookstores. You don't have to have a special box to make a two-for-one offer. An audio tape or CD and a toy that ties in with a children's book are all excellent choices for a two-for-one offer. Again, this approach also works for e-book series. Book one, the older book, sells for $2.99. Book two, the newer book, sells for $3.99. Create a combined e-book version that sells for $5.99. The price combinations can change and increase as you add more books to your series.

Write Another Book

It goes for writers of all genres. The best way to continue selling your first book is to write a second one. I know this can seem more difficult with memoir, but it can still be done.

Make sure when you promote your second book that you always mention your first book. Bring both books with you to those seminars and speaking events, and mention the first book in press releases and during interviews. Writing a second book makes your first book fresh.

Action Item

Don't get discouraged! If your book has a slow sales month, just go back over your list of marketing ideas and start over again.

Resources

Many resources are available for writers, both in print and on the internet. It's not too surprising, I suppose, that writers love to write about writing. Here are some of my favorite resources.

The Craft of Writing

How to Write a Damn Good Novel and *How to Write a Damn Good Novel II,* James N. Frey, published by St. Martin's Press. The best books I've read on the craft of writing fiction. If you'd like to be a better fiction writer, I recommend these books. Nonfiction writers can learn from them, too.

On Writing Well, William Zinsser, published by HarperCollins. An excellent book on the craft of writing.

Inventing the Truth: The Art and Craft of Memoir, William Zinsser, published by Houghton Mifflin Harcourt. Memoir is its own animal, a blend of fiction and nonfiction. If you want to write a memoir, check out this book.

Finish Your Book! A Time Management Guide for Writers, Karen Hodges Miller and Lorette Pruden, published by Open Door Publications. The second book in my own Write Your Book! series offers a number of useful tips on finding the time, the place, and the creative energy needed to finish the book you have always wanted to write.

On Writing, Stephen King, published by Scribner. Whether or not you are a fan of Stephen King's books, *On Writing* is considered by many as one of the best books on the craft of writing.

Style Guides

The Chicago Manual of Style, University of Chicago Press. The final say for all issues of style in book writing.

The Associated Press Stylebook, Basic Books. The essential style guide for newspaper and magazine writers.

Publication Manual of the American Psychological Association, American Psychological Association. The most common guide for the social sciences. Use for academic writing.

AMA Manual of Style, Oxford University Press. An online version is also available at www.amamanualofstyle.com.

The ACS Style Guide: Effective Communication of Scientific Information, American Chemical Society. The guide for science writers.

Finding an Agent

Dozens of websites provide listings for agents. Two that I am most familiar with are:

Poets & Writers: www.pw.org/magazine. This magazine offers excellent information for writers, including a listing of agents in its Tools for Writers section.

Writers' Market: www.writersmarket.com. A resource for writers on a wide variety of topics; it also offers a listing of agents.

Book Proposals

If you plan to look for an agent, you need a book proposal. Here are two excellent resources for nonfiction writers:

Bestselling Book Proposals: The Insider's Guide to Selling Your Work, Rick Frishman and Robyn Freedman Spizman, published by Adam's Media.

How to Write a Book Proposal, Michael Larsen, published by Writer's Digest Books.

Marketing Your Work

Writer's Market. This is the bible for writers and authors. It includes listings for magazines, book publishers, and agents, as well as tips on selling your work. Not only is there a yearly hardcover edition of the main Writer's Market, but there are also special editions for children's writers, poets, novel and short story writers, as well as others.

How to Make Real Money Selling Books (Without Worrying About Returns): A Complete Guide to the Book Publishers' World of Special Sales, Brian Jud, president of Book Marketing Works, a consulting firm established to help independent publishers market their titles to non-bookstore outlets. He is host of the television series The Book Authority and is a regular speaker on marketing topics at Independent Book Publishers Association's (IBPA's) Publishing University.

Dan Poynter's Self-Publishing Manual: How to Write, Print and Sell Your Own Book, Dan Poynter, Para Publishing. A nationally known expert, Poynter has more than a dozen books on writing, publishing, and marketing books.

ADVANTAGE: Harnessing Cumulative Advantage in the Winner Takes All Publishing Market, Joe Solari, explains the marketing theory of cumulative advantage and how you can use it specifically to increase your sales on Amazon.

How to Sell Your Book Today: Focus your book marketing for the new digital economy, Karen Hodges Miller, published by Open Door Publications.

Online Resources

When you're in the middle of writing, you don't want to be interrupted, even by something as simple as checking a spelling or looking up a definition. That's when the internet really helps. Here are some great online resources that make writing just a little easier:

www.dictionary.com There are lots of dictionary sites out there, but I find this one of the easiest to use for a quick spelling or definition check.

www.thesaurus.com Don't depend on the little thesaurus feature you'll find in Microsoft Word. As part of the dictionary.com site, this website makes Roget's complex book obsolete.

www.brainyquote.com This is a feature of Google and one of my favorites. If you need a quote on almost any subject under the sun, you can find it here.

www.grammerly.com A great resource you can add to your software to correct mistakes on the fly. There is a free and a paid version. I use it all the time for emails and business writing. It might be a little annoying, however, for novel writers who may have characters who do not always use the best grammar when they speak. Try it out and see if you like it.

Book Review Sites

There are a number of websites devoted to book reviews. They include both general review sites and sites devoted to specific genres.

www.goodreads.com One of the largest online resources for readers. Its users recommend books, compare what they are reading, keep track of what they've read and would like to read, find their next favorite book, form book clubs, and more. It offers a program for authors to promote their books.

LibraryThing is another member-based review site at http://www.librarything.com/

The Book Trap offers resources for readers at http://thebooktrap.weebly.com/readers-resource/the-midlist

The Indie View offers a very large list of book reviewers at http://www.theindieview.com/indie-reviewers/

Copyright

The U.S. Copyright Office can be found at www.copyright.gov. You'll find a lot of useful information on copyright law. You can also register your book online or file a claim.

E-Book Resources

Kindle Direct Publishing at https://kdp.amazon.com/en_US/ Everything you need to know about publishing an e-book for Amazon Kindle can be found on this site.

https://press.barnesandnoble.com is Barnes & Nobles' site for publishing books for the Nook e-reader.

www.smashwords.com. Read the "How to Publish on Smashwords" section thoroughly before you begin.

www.kobo.com/writinglife. Along with allowing you to upload your book, the Kobo site also offers interesting information.

Websites

Wordpress.com. A good site to host your blog or website.

GoDaddy.com. Purchase your URL, webhosting, and other services.

Silverhoopedge.com. Lisa Snyder of Silver Hoop Edge is my website designer, and I can highly recommend working with her. If you want a custom website, this is the place to go.

Amazon Resources

Maximize your listing at Amazon Author Central.

For information on Amazon reviewers, go to Amazon's

Top Reviewers list at http://www.amazon.com/review/top-reviewers

Other Resources
Bowker Book Services
To obtain an ISBN and barcode and learn about other publishing services, go to www.bowker.com

Keyword Search Sites
If you are having trouble thinking of keywords to use for your website, a number of free keyword generator sites are available online.

www.SEOBook.com: Go to the tools section of this site for the generator.

Grants for Writers
Poets and Writers, a magazine website with a lot more information than just grants, at www.pw.org

Mid-Atlantic Arts Foundation, for writers in the mid-Atlantic area, www.midatlanticarts.org. There are similar organizations in different regions of the country and many states.

Funds for Writers is a good website with a wealth of interesting information at www.fundsforwriters.com

Reposting Sites
A good way to gain more credibility from your blog posts is to repost them to other sites. Here are three popular sites. There are dozens of others.
www.digg.com
www.shewrites.com
www.reddit.com

E-Book Promotions
These sites send out daily newsletters to readers

detailing e-book promotions. Costs vary. I recommend you sign up for a site and use it for a few weeks to understand how it works before you use it for a promotion. Most of the sites listed here require you to have **ten customer reviews on Amazon.**

www.Bookbub.com has one of the largest subscriptions, costs the most, and is the hardest on which to be accepted, but if you do get a promotion on it, you will make back your money.

www.Ereadernewstoday.com A favorite of mine for romance, general fiction, and nonfiction.

Some other sites that authors I know have used successfully are:
www.bargainbooksy.com
www.robinreads.com
www.thefussylibrarian.com

Many other sites out there offer similar services. Don't just stop at this list; go online and research more. Experiment and find out which work the best for you. It is all about finding out which sites your potential readers are using.

Press Releases

Here is the press release I used for my book.

Hibiscus Strong by Karen Hodges Miller:
A Tale of Women's Empowerment and Miami's Vibrant History
FOR IMMEDIATE RELEASE

In a captivating exploration of women's empowerment and familial legacy, author Karen Hodges Miller unveils *Hibiscus Strong,* a compelling collection of short stories that intricately weave together to form a tapestry of resilience and strength across generations. From her great-grandparents to her own childhood, Hodges Miller's latest release offers readers an intimate glimpse into the lives of her ancestors, resonating with the universal themes of perseverance and empowerment.

Karen Hodges Miller's family played a pivotal role in the early development of Miami. Amid the bustling growth of the city, her great-grandfather drove the first train into Miami in 1896, marking a historic moment in the city's history. The family's journey through Miami's formative years brought them into contact with a diverse array of individuals, from Henry Flager, owner of the Florida East Coast Railway, to Julie Tuttle, the "mother of Miami," Dr. James Jackson, Miami's first doctor, to Marjorie Stoneman Douglas and even Al Capone, reflecting the rich tapestry of the city's history.

As Miami emerges as a character in its own right, *Hibiscus Strong* delves deep into the lives of Hodges Miller's family members, crafting a narrative that celebrates the triumphs and challenges faced by women throughout history. Through vivid storytelling and poignant reflections, the book invites readers to journey alongside the author as she uncovers the untold stories of her heritage.

What sets *Hibiscus Strong* apart is its unique structure, seamlessly weaving individual narratives into a cohesive whole. This innovative approach not only engages readers but also underscores the interconnectedness of personal experiences across time and space. As readers immerse themselves in these richly textured tales, they are prompted to reflect on their own familial legacies and the enduring power of storytelling to inspire and uplift.

Karen Hodges Miller's *Hibiscus Strong* stands as a testament to the resilience and indomitable spirit of women across generations. Through her evocative prose and heartfelt storytelling, Hodges Miller offers readers a profound exploration of identity, heritage, and the enduring bonds that unite us all.

For those seeking inspiration, connection, and a deeper understanding of the legacy passed down through family lines, *Hibiscus Strong* is a must-read. The book is available for purchase on Amazon at https://www.amazon.com/Hibiscus-Strong-Karen-Hodges-Miller-ebook/dp/B0CW1GLR15.

For media inquiries or further information, please contact (insert contact information)

Acknowledgments

I want to thank fellow authors and friends, Janice Detrie, Wendy Wyatt, and Sherri A. Lynn for reading everything, sometimes several times, in order to make this the best book possible. They even counted the number of times I used the word "you" and made sure I had not overdone it.

Also, I need to thank Vivan Fransen for proofreading. Vivian, you are the best!

About the Author

Karen Hodges Miller is CEO and publisher at Open Door Publications, a company that specializes in helping authors navigate the world of publishing in the 21st century. The company assists both published and first-time authors with the wide variety of skills and tasks needed to successfully write, publish, and market a book.

Karen herself has written ten books, both fiction and nonfiction, as well as countless newspaper and magazine articles in her 30-year career. Her books on publishing include *How to Sell Your Book Today*, *Self-Publishing: You Can Do This!* and *Authorpreneur: Build the Business Behind the Book.* Her memoir, *Hibiscus Strong*, was published in 2024.

Karen collects websites like most Southern women collect china (jut read her memoir to understand that reference!) You can find out more about her at OpenDoorPublications.com, KarenHodgesMiller.com, at HibiscusStrong.com, and on LinkedIn and Facebook at: facebook.com/OpenDoorPublications.

www.ingramcontent.com/pod-product-compliance
Lightning Source LLC
Chambersburg PA
CBHW060838050426
42453CB00008B/742